# Sense, Nonsense and
# the National Curriculum

## Dedication

To the teachers everywhere and to the professional staff of the National Curriculum Council.

# Sense, Nonsense and the National Curriculum

*Edited by*

Michael Barber and Duncan Graham

 The Falmer Press

(A member of the Taylor & Francis Group)
London • Washington, D.C.

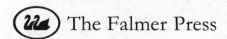

UK      The Falmer Press, 4 John St, London WC1N 2ET
USA     The Falmer Press, Taylor & Francis Inc., 1900 Frost Road, Suite 101, Bristol, PA 19007

---

First published 1993

**A catalogue record of this publication is available from the British Library**

ISBN 0 75070 160 9 cased
ISBN 0 75070 161 7 paperback

**Library of Congress Cataloging-in-Publication Data are available on request**

Jacket design by Caroline Archer

Typeset in 10/12pt Garamond by
Graphicraft Typesetters Ltd., Hong Kong

*Printed in Great Britain by Burgess Science Press, Basingstoke on paper which has a specified pH value on final paper manufacture of not less than 7.5 and is therefore 'acid free'.*

# Contents

# Preface

The National Curriculum has been with us for four years and more. It seems longer. Few would abolish it, but everyone would change it. Teachers have staggered under the workload, worried about the extent of the prescription and the pace with which it has been put in place. From the right and from within the Government it is attacked as representing the work of the education establishment although the facts contradict this. The National Curriculum Council has found itself increasingly the scapegoat for over-ambition, over-design and assessment over the top. Premature changes in the Orders based on opinion, rather than research, have not helped and have raised fundamental questions about whose hand is, and should be, on the tiller.

The editors asked a group of well-known practitioners with different backgrounds, experiences and viewpoints to reflect on the strengths and weaknesses, the gains and losses and for their informed view on the way forward. It should be noted at the outset that the focus has been very much on England, and that the Welsh dimension of the National Curriculum has not been investigated. Readers will find much to stimulate, some things to be pleased about and not a few major concerns. In spite of the diversity, consistent messages appear which we have attempted to draw together at the end. The preceding chapters are arranged to give background and overall perspectives in the first section, front line views in the second and third and challenging looks at the future in the fourth.

The editors would like to thank the contributors for all their good works and Tanya Kreisky and Wendy Graham who transformed piles of untidy paper into measured prose. While the opinions expressed are those of the contributors, we take the blame for errors and omissions.

**Michael Barber**
**Duncan Graham**
*London and Appleby 1992*

# Part 1

## *Perspectives on Implementation*

# Chapter 1

# Reflections on the First Four Years

*Duncan Graham*

Four years on and it is time to draw the first conclusions about the National Curriculum. It will be some time before much that is definitive is said beyond the fact that the principles are now largely unchallenged. Debate centres on detail: no cries for abolition are heard, even from Tim Brighouse! The contributors give assessment from a range of viewpoints which will assist those coping now and no doubt those who will study the nineties in retrospect. The purpose of this chapter is to set the context in which the revolution has taken place; this entails a look at the other changes which have coincided, some by design, many, one suspects, by accident. There are many stables in the Department for Education, but few interconnecting doors. Those of us who have striven to flesh out political assurances that the National Curriculum, TVEI and GCSE were uniquely compatible have cause to smile — albeit between clenched teeth. Currently, the thrust towards specialization of schools sits uncomfortably with the concept of a truly National Curriculum, and with entitlement. The National Curriculum was intended to be relevant in a sense which made academic and vocational GCSEs and so on redundant. It is worth looking back at its genesis before attempting to assess its achievements in terms of relevance, standards, progression, differentiation, entitlement and the rest.

The declared agenda for the National Curriculum has a number of aspects. One was to diminish the patchiness which was widely seen to bedevil the English system, the most decentralized of all. Its disadvantages were now seen to outweigh the benefits of initiative at local level. Entitlement was implied, although not spoken of by ministers. It was, perhaps, too egalitarian a concept, and had worrying resource implications. There was a thrust towards making the curriculum more relevant. This reflects the long-standing debate on the nature of education in England. Growing doubt about the Romantic approach, rather than the teutonic practical, were reinforced by the international tendency in the eighties to see education in terms of its economic utility. Contrasts between the economic performances of the USA and Europe, when set against the emergent nations, led to a whole new approach. In

England it came late in the guise of the Tory Modernists, led by David (later Lord) Young. The creation of the Manpower Services Commission (MSC) with the active support of the then Secretary of State for Education and Science, Sir Keith Joseph, had a profound effect. There was the Technical and Vocational Education Initiative (TVEI), which did more to change secondary teaching than had anything for years. As a by-product, the success of the MSC in interventionism did not pass unnoticed in the DES.

There was, too, the Great Standards Debate. This tends to be endemic and is probably an intergenerational phenomenon, reinforced in the UK by the gulf between businesspeople and educationalists about the basics. The eighties saw a positive deluge of comparisons which invariably showed up the UK as falling behind in numeracy and literacy. Whatever the arguments about the accuracy and relevance of these, public perceptions were influenced. As I said at the time, there was certainly no evidence coming through that standards were too high.

The hidden agenda had much to do with a volatile combination of political distrust of teachers, and public concern about teaching methods. While (as usual) teaching in most places was varied and balanced, verging on the conservative, the headlines in the tabloids and the heavies focussed on the extremists, those who had taken learning by enjoyment, pupil-centred learning, reading by osmosis, and so on, to extremes, turning respectable practices in aggregate image into something parents did not understand or like the sound of. It followed, therefore, that what was to be taught would be laid down in unique detail — the adjective is used in its literal sense. Testing would be on an unprecedented scale, and trust of teachers was not a built-in feature. There were two paradoxes, which say much for the skill of civil servants, and the moderating influence of Kenneth Baker. One was that methodology was excluded from prescription by the Government in the Act, as was the time to be allocated to each subject. The birthright of the profession is under more threat now, perhaps, than it was then. Equally surprisingly, the philosophy of testing laid upon the Schools Examination and Assessment Council (SEAC) was liberal and well-intentioned, far from the short sharp tests one might have anticipated. Oddly enough, these good intentions, enshrined in the Task Group on Assessment and Testing (TGAT) report, bore the seeds of disaster for testing and, at times, it seemed, for the National Curriculum itself. If it was not possible to trust teachers as partners, then ambitions should have been scaled down — my own behind-the-scenes advocacy was for a simple system which put pressure on schools to improve standards and expectations, was diagnostically useful, and gave parents more helpful information. We may get to this, the way things are going.

Another underlying factor was the anti local government sentiment which the Government has consistently exhibited since 1979. Whatever the alleged shortcomings in local government, they had been largely removed by the late eighties — the party had long been over. Local government was, by any measure, palpably more efficient than central in terms of cost effectiveness.

One reason for a National Curriculum must have been to have secure central control, when increased discretion was to be given to 25,000 schools, at the expense of LEAs.

Looking back, one can see the interplay of declared and hidden agendas. The needs of the nation, the acknowledged deficiencies were subsumed in the Baker vision — he deserves credit for that. They were, to an extent, hijacked by the Tory 'traditional right', Victorian values brigade, by the centralists, and, no doubt, by the DES, stung by the jibes of the MSC. When last had an education initiative required a DES staff increase, some drawn from other departments? The stage was set.

Was it all necessary? It is probable that it was more so politically than in terms of the education of the nation. In the decade since 1980, pressures on the education service had brought change. An event seldom mentioned was the appearance of *DES Circular 6/81*. This was the one which required LEAs to have and to declare a curriculum policy. Some may have been surprised to find that they were responsible for the curriculum. Most responded so copiously that a room in Elizabeth House had to be set aside for the responses, pending a decision on what to do with them. They need not have worried. LEAs and schools made massive strides in defining and implementing their policies. Combined with sterling work by LEAs and their advisers on inspection and quality assurance, and the agreement, although not sadly then, the implementation, of a National Appraisal Scheme, the evidence is that the desired improvements were in train. That there was a degree of shooting behind the target was due to a lack of political perceptiveness as much as the failure of the education service to publicize its successes.

Was it a revolution? The answer must be yes, for a number of reasons. It did not come from the education industry, rather from the commercial one. No one has yet admitted to inventing Attainment Targets and Programmes of Study. They came unsullied by classroom practice or by any kind of research base. It can be argued that it would not have been accomplished any other way. Equally novel was the approach used in tackling subject content. The membership of the working groups may initially have seemed orthodox enough: after all I did (eventually) chair the mathematics group. But the remit was revolutionary — a quick pragmatic assessment of what the nation expected in each subject at ages 7, 11, 14 and 16, ensuring good practice as defined by the group, and with minimal consultation. One of the enigmas — even embarrassments for some — is that it worked so well. Little controversy has arisen over content. There is too much of it, but of course no subject enthusiast will sell their subject short. Working groups in which zealots outnumber cynics are never knowingly undersold. Less revolutionary was the subject approach and the choice thereof. Areas of experience, so beloved by HMI, had not caught on sufficiently to prevent a tide of nostalgic subjectism, backed by traditional baronies, from holding sway. The subjects could have come from Kenneth Baker's prep school prospectus!

Revolutionary too was the sheer scale, scope and detail of the thing. No other National Curriculum, to my knowledge, comes near to it. It is the cause of grudging admiration abroad, but not to the point of emulation. The same is clearly true of the testing monster which was created — a revolution which came near to causing a revolution — in schools.

In aggregate, the implications added up to the abandonment, after 120 years of state education, of the traditional freedoms and their replacements by compulsion with the full force of the law behind it. The power for good, the potential, was enormous. If implemented sympathetically it could confirm good schools in their practice without constraining them. It could level up: it did little credit to the minority of independent school heads who claimed that it would level down. Perhaps they feared the competition. It also created the potential for great misuse of power. Central statutory detailed control of the curriculum is a heady brew for politicians. Not all, as we have seen, can resist the temptation. It can also cause fright. The price of entitlement is constraint. Some of those who had demanded detailed prescription changed their minds when they saw the consequences. It was from the Acts progenitors that the cries about complexity and over-prescription were heard most clearly. The scapegoats were to be the National Curriculum Council (NCC) and the SEAC, notwithstanding that they were created by the very same Act which set down the blueprint long before they put their plates up in York and Notting Hill Gate.

In setting in context the front-line contributions which make this book so fascinating, it will be useful to analyze the successes and failures as they appear now, but to do so in the light of other developments which have had an impact.

Had the National Curriculum had a free run, perhaps the only other projects being teacher appraisal and reconciliation with GCSE and post-16 education, then more substantial progress would have been made. It was not to be. There were other initiatives almost as fundamental, and there has been a failure to restore the partnerships which all of us initially saw as so obviously necessary. The National Curriculum can be explained as shock therapy for the system. That can only work once and for a limited period. By such means you can galvanize but not convert. In return for manfully shouldering the burdens, teachers had a right to expect a renewed share in curriculum development, albeit in partnership with others. The concentration of power in political hands, and sadly the politicization of the NCC and the SEAC has prevented this from coming about.

The suspicion about teachers has broadened into an all-embracing distaste for professionals as a whole. While their views should never be taken as gospel, it is well to take account of their expertise and experience. The trouble comes when that advice, as in the nature of things, urges caution consultation and easing the timetable. This is construed as lack of dedication and commitment, a desire to obstruct the speedy implementation of the latest good idea. We seem to have lost for the time being the mutual trust which is so essential. A good illustration lies in the coursework saga. You will recall the ministers sought to reduce it for reasons which perhaps were less than logical. Be that as it may, the chopping and changing caused as much damage and confusion as the change in policy itself. By that time, the voice of professional advisers was at best muted.

Another difficult factor was the divisions and rivalries at the centre of events. Disraeli spoke of politics as a 'greasy pole', up and down which the warring factions slithered. The DES initially climbed up with the National Curriculum — the direct participatory control of the curriculum garden at last. By the same token, HMI began their inexorable decline. Without exclusive rights, as it were, they were threatened. New boys on the pole were the NCC and the SEAC — a threat to both the established players. They were quangoes, which civil servants dislike, had powers which were ill-defined, and had difficult, if not impossible, tasks to undertake. It will take time to come to a final conclusion about the end product. I suspect that all the parties will be seen to have lost — even the DES whose officers chose to become 'professionals' just before the extinction of the species. The politicization of the NCC and the SEAC bodes ill for their future as credible independent holders of the ring. The proposal in the Current Education Bill for a School Curriculum and Assessment Authority under the tight direction of the Secretary of State provides little comfort. One upshot of all this is that an awful lot of energy which could have gone into implementing the National Curriculum more effectively was diverted into disputation and wrangling. Perhaps when the final balance sheet is drawn, the most damaging development of all will be seen to have been the appearance of a black hole in the field of quality assurance or control. The expectation in 1988 was that, apart from the NCC, the traditional guardians of quality — HMI and LEAs and their advisers — would play a major role in ensuring quality implementation and the monitoring of standards. Instead, their influence has waned significantly: it seems unlikely that the combining of their resources, which many have advocated, will now take place. They could have been the backbone of a system in which various groups contributed to the overall plan. Separately, these do not add up; making it easier to say who cannot do the job than who can. Schools cannot do it alone. They need comparative judgment, their own assessments inevitably appear incestuous. It cannot be governors and parents. They are key players, but not alone. Experience suggests that, left to it, they will narrow the curriculum and stifle initiatives in methodology. It cannot be crude result and league tables. The miracle here is that something so discredited and demonstrably unfair can have had such a long shelf life. Politicians are drawn to the cheap and the simple. That is not to say that publication of results, with fair comparisons, should not take place.

Assessment cannot just be by the consumers — business and commerce — their needs are too ill-defined and diverse. Least of all, in my view, can it be inspection as laid down in the 1992 Act. Inspection and judgment cannot take place in a vacuum, without background knowledge and support. Good schools, and bad, will delight in a mixture of whitewash and wool over eyes.

The plan lacks credibility: it is an insult to all those who have worked over the years to develop sensitive and constructive performance indicators. It is completely lacking in a 'bottom-up' component in which schools assess themselves against criteria and gain recognition through accreditation. What is needed is the right combination of all of the ingredients. They do not of themselves constitute a recipe.

The last of the negative factors has been lack of resources. The chapter contributed by John Atkins makes compulsive reading. Once all the arguments about resources not being the only factor in progress have been heard, it remains true that we have had a National Curriculum on the cheap. Inspection will be on the cheap too, which is poetic justice in a way. But the funds set aside for training, particularly on assessment, have been woefully inadequate. The rise in class sizes and pupil : teacher ratios is little short of disastrous. The National Curriculum rightly emphasizes the individual pupil in both attainment and assessment. There is known argument that this requires fewer, rather than more, teachers. Investment in books and materials, and in accommodation, has followed the dismal pattern. Most damaging of all is that disparities in resources have been accentuated rather than narrowed. Quite apart from the effects of CTCs and opting out, the increasing pressure on parents to contribute towards essentials has militated against the disadvantaged getting the full benefits of the entitlement. It is to be hoped that governors, as they see the inadequacies, will wield effective pressure. They must speak up now as LEAs lose their power to even out the disparities. The National Curriculum holds out great prospects to those who traditionally gain least help from our system. It has yet to be realized.

Here is a personal assessment of successes and failures so far, as a yardstick for comparison with the conclusions drawn from different viewpoints by the contributors. There are many things on which there is a measure of consensus. One is that the National Curriculum is worth persevering with. On balance, it has proved better to have it. In terms of content we have a clear definition which is broadly accepted. It is probably too much, although it will be difficult to reduce, as distinct from rearrange. Although ministers bang on about over-prescription, the recent revisions in maths and science did not reduce it at all; it simplified a bit which was no more than helpful. The really exciting prospect lies in the hands of schools. The content need not be delivered in subject form — 'throwing all the Attainment Targets on the floor' and reassembling them could, at a stroke, reduce overlap, volume and pressure. It could also put some excitement back. The first signs are there.

A real success has been the preservation and enhancement of the whole curriculum. In *Curriculum Guidance 3* (1989), the NCC provided a working definition of it as the ten subjects, RE, additional subjects at Key Stage 4 and Dimensions, Skills and Themes. A right-wing attempt to restrict it to the statutory provision was thwarted — the NCC'S finest hour? There is solid evidence of breadth and balance being maintained and strengthened in schools, and the fear that only the examined would survive has not been realized.

However, that is a constant battle requiring eternal vigilance. Much still remains to be done in broader areas of equal opportunities and multicultural education. Gender bias in curriculum choice and content has been much reduced: in attitudinal terms there is a long way to go.

A qualified success has been in the field of testing and examinations. At great cost to teachers in time and effort, the curriculum has survived the testing, which has been simplified and made less ambitious. What effect this has had on standards remains an open question. The battle continues with not enough willingness yet to trust teacher assessment. Perhaps the longer term solution lies in a rigorous accreditation of schools, allowing them to test and examine under license. None of this may happen if the desire for simple class-room testing leads to a more old-fashioned approach. In spite of all the evidence that formal examinations are less accurate predictors, the nation has a love affair with them — in a survey, the less successful adults were at them, the more they wanted them for the next generation. For as long as we persist with the quaintness of the 'A' level system and the anachronism of terminal examinations at 16, we are likely to have formal testing from the age of 7.

What of standards? The evidence drawn from the NCC and HMI reports is as encouraging as one would wish at this stage. There is a slow upward trend: one could ask for no more, except the resources to accelerate the process. The curriculum is clearly now more relevant — most if not all of the clutter and lumber has gone, and practice is much more clearly related to realism. Curriculum organization and planning, particularly in primary schools, has improved beyond recognition — it hangs together in terms of progression — no more 'Vikings' every year in primaries! In terms of differentiation, evidence is less clear: awareness has been raised, if not yet practice. The signs of rising standards presumably mean a rise in expectations. There is probably more to do here than anywhere else — under-performance is still a national disease. The stark contrast with the emergent nations persists.

The picture as regards teaching methods is, on the whole, encouraging. Diversity has not been diminished; no straitjackets have been imposed. What has happened is that teachers have become infinitely more aware of the strengths and limitations of different methods. Project and topic methods are used more effectively by those who recognize how they should be augmented by class teaching and more formal methods. A great delight for me recently has been to sit in on analytical staff room debates of a quality unknown ten years ago. The downside is the constant threat of external pressure to revert solely to formal class teaching. It will probably be more difficult to experiment in the future. The traditionalist will welcome this, but one wonders if teaching methods in the twenty-first century should not be very different from those of the late 19th. I wonder if governing bodies will allow the clean slate approach which is producing stimulating new ideas in the USA. Whatever happens here, at least classrooms are wide open to inspection and discussion. The strength of teacher appraisal lies in classroom observation.

Now for the downside. Resources, quality assurance, special needs and equal opportunities have already been mentioned. The biggest single worry must lie in the potential for political interference. It is inherent in a National Curriculum. Kenneth Baker and John MacGregor recognized this and knew the delicate line between general concern and detailed involvement. Kenneth Clarke had fewer inhibitions, as his incursions into history show. There is a need to thrash out a set of rules which allow for politicians and educationalists to meet on constructive terms. This should be accompanied by the depoliticization of the NCC and SEAC. Impartial professional advice is at a premium.

Another casualty has been that of proper independent research, evaluation and monitoring. The NCC was not permitted to undertake the broad, disinterested research which I envisaged when appointed. Changing and updating of the curriculum needs to be on the best available evidence, commissioned from reputable bodies. Maths and science are cases in point. The 1991 revisions simplified them, but at the expense of the improvements a more organized scrutiny would undoubtedly have produced. It may have been worth taking the shock approach in 1988 over the National Curriculum. That must not become a way of life. There is every reason to fear that changes will be made in the Orders in English and Technology without proper debate and consultation. Where is the evidence that the English Orders have not worked well? By whose whim is Technology to revert to the orthodoxy of the fifties and sixties?

Looking back over the four years, it is likely that more good than harm has come from the introduction of the National Curriculum. If I am tempted to go for the Scottish 'not proven' verdict, it is only because the next stage will depend heavily on some simple but essential things. These are a more genuine partnership, sound and reasoned change, political distancing from the detail of the curriculum, and adequate resources. In addition, we need a quality assurance system involving all the interested parties, a range of methods, and coherent organization. How odd if there were to be no credible method of answering the standards question by the mid-nineties. Shades of the seventies and eighties!

*Chapter 2*

# Teachers and the National Curriculum: Learning to Love It?

*Michael Barber*

There is a famous tale told by R.A. Butler in his memoirs. In offering him the post of President of the Board of Education, Churchill urged, 'I should be grateful if you could introduce a note of patriotism into the schools . . . Tell the children that Wolfe won Quebec'. Butler hesitated. This was not the sort of thing Presidents of the Board of Education did. 'I don't mean by instruction' explained Churchill, 'but by example'. This appears to have been the only curriculum-related instruction issued by the Prime Minister of the most overtly interventionist Government of the twentieth century. Fifty years on, a Government which claims to have spent a decade rolling back the frontiers of the state is not only prescribing in detail what should be taught and how it should be assessed, it is also exercising its powers to intervene in response to short-term political considerations. Viewed from the broad historical perspective, this is richly ironic. More importantly, it is also a cause of continuing confusion and uncertainty among teachers. Whether or not they have been persuaded that the National Curriculum of today is a good thing (and there is evidence that broadly they have), their commitment is tempered by the fear of intervention and change of direction tomorrow.

This chapter examines how teachers have responded to the Government's National Curriculum plans over the last five years. It then assesses the extent to which the profession has gone beyond response, to articulate an alternative strategy for the curriculum.

## The Historical Context

The current contest over the National Curriculum can be isolated neither from its historical origins, nor from the much wider educational conflict which has characterized the 1980s. These factors set the context for the current conflict over the curriculum. Historically, conflict between the Government and teachers over the curriculum is nothing new. It took the National Union of

Teachers twenty-five years from its foundation in 1870 to overthrow the hated system of payment by results, under which the government had specified annually what it expected should be learnt. Inspectors, 'young men fresh from university who had never seen the inside of an elementary school', (quoted in Barber, 1992, p. 7) then checked whether teachers had been successful. The school's grant and hence the teacher's salary depended on the outcome of this inspection.

In the twenty or thirty years following the demise of this draconian system, a pragmatic compromise was reached. The Government would prevent teachers from becoming excessively integrated in the labour movement by allowing them extensive control over the curriculum and a substantial degree of stability. Elementary education, to most of the ruling class, was designed to do no more than promote learning of the 3Rs and some Victorian moral values. It would be kept in its place by tight restrictions on public expenditure and by keeping it separate as far as possible from the 'public' schools and secondary grammar schools which provided access to power and the professions for the children of the upper and middle classes. This, as Lord Eustace Percy, President of the Board of Education in the late 1920s, characterized it, was indirect rule similar to that designed by Lord Lugard to rule Nigeria.

Fascism and war brought change. The 1944 Education Act established secondary education for all and laid the basis for a newly unified teaching profession. Apart from its broad requirement, echoed later by the 1988 Act that:

> ... it shall be the duty of the local education authority for every area, so far as their powers extend, to contribute towards the spiritual, moral, mental and physical development of the community ... (1944 Education Act, Section 7)

it had nothing to say about the curriculum. The lesson of fascism, as Churchill's conversation with Butler reveals, was that state interference in the curriculum was dangerous. This became a shibboleth among teachers. As Ronald Gould, General Secretary of the NUT, put it,

> It have heard it said that the existence in this country of 146 strong, vigorous LEAs safeguards democracy and lessens the risk of dictatorship ... an even greater safeguard is the existence of a quarter of a million teachers who are free to decide what should be taught and how it should be taught. (quoted in Barber, 1992, p. 135)

When, in the early 1960s, the then Conservative Government proposed the establishment of a curriculum study group within the DES, Gould attacked it on precisely these grounds. The Minister's proposal was a threat to democracy. What emerged was the Schools' Council, possibly Gould's idea, on which there would be a teacher majority. For the next two decades, the curriculum work of the NUT and other teacher organizations focused on the Schools'

Council. Out of it emerged some highly significant national developments, such as the Schools' Council History Project, but perhaps above all the growth of a culture of school-based curriculum development. The parallel growth of mode 3 CSEs with their emphasis on school-designed syllabuses reinforced this process. The Schools' Council proved far less successful, partly because of its philosophical approach, in bringing about either national consensus on the scope and content of the curriculum or much needed reform of examinations at 16.

The growing concern of the Government and the wider public about education standards following the seismic economic shocks of the seventies, combined with this apparent failure to provide the framework for 1980s debate on the curriculum. Between James Callaghan's Ruskin speech in 1976, and the White Paper, *Better Schools*, in 1985, the Government moved cautiously towards a nationally defined curriculum. As Stephen Ball and others have shown, there were differences of emphasis between the DES and HMI, particularly over whether traditional subjects should form the basis of the National Curriculum. Significantly, however, once the Schools' Council had been abolished and replaced by much weaker Government-nominated bodies, there was no national forum in which the professional voice on the curriculum could be heard. Alan Evans, then Head of Education at the NUT, advocated the establishment by teacher organizations and LEAs of a curriculum council of their own, but was unable to generate sufficient support. Given the exploitation of this vacuum by the Government in the years that followed, the foresight of Evans' proposal is clearly recognizable.

The NUT's response to *Better Schools* probably represents the advanced professional thinking of the time.

> The National Union of Teachers has viewed with concern the attempts made by Government to exert an influence over the curriculum of schools. That concern is heightened when the Union considers the direction in which that influence is being exerted.

There is a strong echo of Gould here. While the comment acknowledges that 'a common curriculum for most of the period of compulsory schooling' would be beneficial, it argues, with a degree of contradiction, that 'the Government's attempt to define the curriculum nationally is misconceived'. Instead, it argues for a broad agreement about aims.

The response gave priority to a demolition of the predilection of the Government in the Keith Joseph era for vocational education and skills training. It is fascinating that in 1985 the Union attacked the Government for overemphasis on 'the learning process' and for forgetting that 'knowledge has an intrinsic value'. Five years later, the Government was fixated on knowledge rather than the learning process to a level reminiscent of Thomas Gradgrind.

In fact, *Better Schools* was mild in its prescriptions compared to what emerged under Kenneth Baker from 1987 onwards. The patient approach of the preceding decade was swept away. The advocates of subjects in the DES had routed the HMI advocates of 'areas of experience', and the teaching profession, battered and bruised after three years of conflict over salaries, was in retreat. By contrast, the Government had the added confidence it derived from a resounding election victory in June of that year.

## The Educational Context

The newly-elected Conservative Government set out not only to introduce a National Curriculum but also to bring about the most wide-ranging reform of the education system since the war. Many of the contributions to this book bear eloquent testimony to the consequences of the Education Reform Act at all levels in the system: national, local and school. In the lived experience of people working in the education system, it is simply impossible to analyze the National Curriculum in isolation from all the other aspects of reform. In a book designed to examine the impact of the National Curriculum, the other reforms must at least be acknowledged, if not analyzed. Delegated budgets, formula-funding based on pupil numbers, and open enrolment have created an educational market in which schools must compete for pupils. The option of grant-maintained status or City Technology Colleges creates diversity and clearly favours some at the expense of the rest. In market terminology, they offer a differentiated product. In parallel, responsibility for the pay, conditions of service and tenure of teachers have become increasingly the responsibility of school governing bodies rather than LEAs or central government. Government plans to shift the emphasis in initial teacher education towards schools and to break the inspection monopolies of HMI and LEA inspectors are consistent with this market orientation.

The National Curriculum and Assessment must be seen as part of this grand design. They have a dual function. Firstly, while the rest of the reform agenda atomises, splinters and divides (albeit under the watchful gaze of a Secretary of State with a raft of powers to alter the rules without legislation); the National Curriculum centralizes, holds together and stresses uniformity. Secondly, by specifying in detail what must be taught and how it should be tested and by requiring the publication of those results, the Government is able to provide the basis for parents to make comparisons and thus make an informed market choice. The objection that raw test results lead to misinformed choice has so far been dismissed as professionals complicating the issue, though by the end of 1992, Government thinking appeared to be shifting.

Two further factors influencing the context need to be taken into account. Firstly, the implementation process has been notable for its haste, the absence of serious consultation with teachers, and a failure to provide the necessary resources. John Atkins' chapter demonstrates the latter starkly.

Secondly, and perhaps more profoundly, taken together the reforms reveal a deeper conflict. Ultimately at stake is the nature of teaching and the professionalism of teachers. In spite of high sounding words in some DES publications and ministerial speeches, the Government's conception of teachers rejects notions of professional autonomy, discretion or even judgment and casts teachers instead as messengers, passing on the knowledge in the National Curriculum to serried ranks of (increasingly large) classes of pupils. To be sure this is a caricature, but the conflict over the professional role in my view helps to explain the bitter resentment of teachers for the Government, not to mention the drop-out rate from the profession.

The truly startling fact given this context is that the National Curriculum, and indeed some of the other reforms, have been implemented with a substantial degree of success. There are three reasons for this, each of them deeply ironic. One is that LEAs, on the whole, have provided effective assistance, support and training to schools, yet their continued existence remains doubtful. All the evaluations of National Curriculum implementation are strongly positive about the role LEAs, and particularly their advisory or curriculum support teachers, have played. The second is that in spite of the inevitable criticism that a Government-appointed quango was bound to attract, the National Curriculum Council has shown a high degree of professionalism and won the grudging respect of teachers. The same cannot be said of SEAC which has suffered from greater political direction and a series of misjudgments over assessment of 7-year-olds. (No wonder that at a recent informal discussion among teacher union representatives about a possible merger of NCC and SEAC, one remarked wrily that 'the only aspect of SEAC worth preserving is its cheeseboard', which, to those who attend meetings there, has become legendary.)

The third and most important reason for relative success has been the skills and professionalism of teachers. This too is acknowledged in HMI and other evaluations of National Curriculum implementation. It is the deepest irony of all that the success of reforms implemented by a Government which challenges the concept of teachers as professionals has depended precisely on their professional skills developed and refined in a preceding, more liberal era. Whether, if the current philistinism were to be perpetuated, the system could implement a major structural reform ten years from now must be doubtful, but that is to jump ahead of our story.

## The Response to the National Curriculum

When Kenneth Baker's consultation document was published at the start of the 1987 summer holiday, asking for responses soon after it, it was evident that the achievement of agreement with the teaching profession was accorded little priority. It is not surprising that the NUT's response, like those of other teacher organizations, gave prominence to criticism of the lack of consultative mechanisms. It concluded:

> The failure to include representative teachers in (National Curriculum subject working) groups removes any breath of accountability and is a damaging insult to the profession.

It repeated an offer made earlier in the year.

> (The Union) has participated actively in the creation of the consensus which has emerged about the curriculum ... agreement about a National Curriculum now exists and with it a readiness to accept the interests of parents, industry and the community at large in what is taught ... The Union believes that the nation depends ultimately upon the integrity of those who guard its professions ... who cannot abdicate from responsibility for decisions made. To that extent what is taught in schools must depend upon teachers. The Union would be very happy to discuss a National Curriculum within these parameters.

It was too late; neither the Union's role nor its proposed parameters were recognized by the Government. In spite of the series of pertinent criticisms which professional organizations made of specific aspects of them, the Government's plans went ahead broadly unaltered. The fact that many of the problems that have since emerged were identified during the 1987 consultation exercise is no comfort to the profession.

By Easter 1988, the NUT was claiming credit for its 'contribution towards building the almost universal educational consensus against the details of Kenneth Baker's proposals for the content and assessment of a National Curriculum'. Instead, it was arguing, as HMI had done a decade earlier, for an entitlement curriculum which 'would aim to provide people with the knowledge, experience, skills and attitudes they need to participate in ... society ...' (Interim Memorandum to NUT Conference 1988). In short, the principle of a National Curriculum had been conceded.

Still contested were its nature and content, the means by which it should be assessed and the process by which these critical decisions should be made. In the short term, the Government had its way on each of these issues. The process was soon established. Subject working groups, made up of people nominated by the Secretary of State, were set up in each of the subjects. Maths, English and science came first. Technology, modern foreign languages, history and geography followed. PE, art and music came at the end, their place in the pecking order firmly established. The reports of each of these groups were put out for consultation by the National Curriculum Council (whose members were also nominated by the Secretary of State), which examined responses and then made recommendations to the Secretary of State. He then laid orders before Parliament. Thus, although there was a consultative process, the Secretary of State had several levers of control. The only check was that if his orders varied from NCC recommendations, he had to explain why. Given the Government's contempt for professional opinion, this proved no stumbling block to political interference.

Three factors require comment; firstly, in spite of the Secretary of State's monopoly on appointments, deep divisions within subject groups became apparent. Secondly, in spite of the exclusion of teachers, the working groups came closer than might have been expected to achieving professional credibility. Thirdly, the subject by subject approach led predictably to a content overload, which is still perhaps the major professional concern over the National Curriculum.

The Mathematics Working Group reveals the first point most vividly. Here the clash between traditionalists and progressives became so bitter that the original Chairman resigned and was replaced by Duncan Graham. His success in banging heads together perhaps contributed to his appointment as the first Chairman and Chief Executive of the National Curriculum Council. The Mathematics National Curriculum proved largely uncontentious once it was published. Only later, when different patterns of attainment had appeared in other subjects, did the need for revision of mathematics become obvious. Even then, its programmes of study were left unchanged. The extent to which the working group in mathematics drew on important earlier work, above all the Cockroft Report, was a significant factor in its success.

The same was true of English, which best illustrates the working group's level of success in achieving a professional consensus. When that champion of tradition, Brian Cox, was appointed to chair the working group, many in the profession feared the worst. In fact, Cox's report drew heavily on the earlier work of the Kingman Committee and proposed a curriculum structure which has breadth and balance and won the consent, and even the admiration, of most English teachers. The fact that, in the summer of 1992, it was under attack from Government ministers is due not to professional or parental concern, but to ministerial obsession and prejudice. Unfortunately, with the curriculum powers of the Education Reform Act behind him, the Secretary of State can enforce his prejudices on every schoolchild in the country.

The problem of curriculum overload emerged inevitably as each of the subject groups staked their territorial claim on the limited curriculum time available. Soon after the Science National Curriculum was implemented, I remember a Head of Science claiming he had solved the overload problem because he had been able to farm out some of the programmes of study and attainment to other subjects, such as geography. Of course, he had, until the other subjects came on stream and wanted to farm out attainment targets of their own. The overload problem is most acute at Key Stages 2 and 4.

Previously, Key Stage 2 was taught according to the tenets of good primary practice: a thematic approach and a focus on the basics of maths and English. Fitting the highly specific subject content of the National Curriculum into that style of curriculum was philosophically repugnant and practically very difficult. Each class teacher found him/herself obliged to know hundreds of statements of attainment in nine subjects (ten in Wales with Welsh). Without training and support, this was mind-boggling. Even with sufficient training, the practicalities of what is expected would be impossible. There was also the consequence such prescription would have on teachers' motivation. Teachers realized this early on. In its response, for example, to the final report of the History Working Group, the NUT argued:

> By far the most serious problem the report presents for the profession is the extent of prescription. It lays down the detail of the history curriculum to an extent which surely serves no purpose, which is educationally unjustifiable and is likely to have a significant negative impact on the motivation of teachers . . .

The particular danger at Key Stage 2 was the consequence such prescription would have for following up local history. Again, the NUT made the point:

> Primary schools, with generally close links with their locality, should be encouraged to make use of the resources in the community. Visits from, or recordings of, adults . . . can provide exciting stimulus for historical study.

Many other representatives of teachers made a similar case. The National Curriculum does not prevent such good practice, but the burden of its content has the double effect of over-filling curriculum time and providing teachers, particularly during the implementation phase, with an excessive burden. Both the Assistant Masters and Mistresses Association (AMMA) and the NUT have separately commissioned studies showing that primary teachers were working over fifty hours a week in 1991. The NUT-commissioned work (see the chapter by John Atkins) found, in addition, that the excessive content requirements had caused a cut in the time children were spending learning basic numeracy and literacy. If teachers' workload cuts no ice with the Government, the evidence of damage to the basics should cause it great anxiety.

The problems at Key Stage 4 were equally predictable. How could a compulsory ten-subject (eleven in Wales) National Curriculum be consistent with the recently introduced GCSE exam for which pupils normally chose between seven and nine subjects? Various solutions to this problem were promoted and dropped before Kenneth Clarke decided that art and music would become optional, and PE 'particularly flexible' after 14. Technology and modern foreign languages would remain compulsory, but not necessarily in GCSE form. Students could opt between history and geography or do a combined course. Only the core of maths, science and English was untouched. This solution was confused, but manageable: it also spelt the end of a balanced and broadly-based National Curriculum through to 16.

The National Curriculum Council appears to its credit to have registered the profession's concerns about Key Stages 2 and 4. Its Corporate Plan, 1992–95, published in December 1991, announced:

> Council will examine the intellectual rationale which has been struck between knowledge, skills and understanding and the demand which the Orders make on pupils . . .

It also asks, quaintly, 'Do the Orders need simplifying in the interests of manageability?'

The same document also made clear that the NCC intended to look at the 14–19 curriculum as a whole, and established a committee to examine the issues. At least, therefore, the crucial problem of Key Stages 2 and 4 are on the agenda. It remains to be seen what the solutions will be. There has been widespread consultation during 1992 on Key Stage 2. However, nothing has yet emerged proposing changes on either issue and there are rumours of deadlock in NCC deliberation, which in any case takes place constantly in the shadow of the politicians.

## The Response to Assessment

While the curriculum unfolded with varying degrees of controversy, the means of assessing it were being developed elsewhere. In fact, it was Kenneth Baker's Task Group of Assessment and Testing, chaired by Professor Paul Black, which had given shape to the National Curriculum. The 1988 Act required there to be programmes of study and attainment targets. It was the TGAT Report that introduced the ten-levels. While much of its advice on testing has been ignored subsequently, the ten-level structure remains firmly in place. Each subject is built around it. Critics hesitate to comment on it, lest a breath of criticism should bring down the house of cards. Yet it builds in some contradictions which, while not yet readily apparent, are accidents waiting to happen. In this year's Key Stage 1 SATS, for example, a substantial number of 7-year-olds have recorded level 4: this is the same level that will represent the lowest grade that can be awarded on a GCSE certificate. To what extent are these levels 4 of respectively a 7-year-old and a 16-year-old comparable? And what will a parent think if their level 4 7-year-old has only progressed, say, to level 7 (good enough for GCSE Grade C) by the age of 14? Three levels in seven years, when they achieved four levels in infant school, will seem meagre progress. Worse still, there was never any attempt to ensure that levels were compatible across subjects. The rationale for the levels in each of the subjects is, in any case, quite different. If parents discover that their 14-year-old daughter is level 6 in everything except, say, technology, they are likely to be concerned about either the school's teaching or the daughter's performance in that subject. Will they be reassured to be told that it's not either, but rather a design flaw in the National Curriculum? Dramas of this sort are likely to begin to unfold in the next two or three years. The publication of results will give them added spice. A junior school will be thrown into a paroxysm of anxiety by receiving too many 'level 4s' at the age of 8. What chance do they have of making significant progress through the levels during Key Stage 2, and if they do, what need will there be for secondary education at all? After all, a level 7 would be a good grade at GCSE.

These problems of the assessment framework lie in the future. The controversies about the design of assessment are already blazing. GCSE has been steadily undermined by the need to mesh it with the National Curriculum and by the politicians' determination to undermine coursework. John Major's speech to the Centre for Policy Studies in July 1991 heralded restrictions in coursework which vary from subject to subject but limit most to 20 per cent. The surprise is the lack of controversy this has caused, probably because the system is facing so many radical changes that it is hard to find the energy to resist all of them. There may also be private relief for some teachers at the reduction in the marking load that John Major's ante-diluvian education attitudes will bring.

The most prominent controversy, however, has been over tests for 7-year-olds. A pilot set of SATs in 2 per cent of primary schools in 1990 proved disastrously misconceived. They almost entirely replaced the curriculum for the first half of the summer term. Those involved in their development went back to the drawing board and redesigned their tests for 1991 when all 7-year-olds were tested for the first time. Once again, test design proved ill-judged. While the content of the tests was generally sound from an educational point of view, once again the time they would take was massively underestimated. Instead of the thirty hours SEAC said they should take, an NUT survey found most classes spent more than fifty hours on them.

In the aftermath, the Government was forced to admit the misjudgment. In any case, pressure from teachers for a reduction in the time and workload demanded by SATs was consistent with demands from the right for simple paper and pencil tests.

The 1992 tests are indeed simpler and more manageable. Nevertheless, teachers still find them abhorrent, as a joint NUT/University of Leeds survey has found. This is partly because they fear the educational consequences of labelling children and schools, but also because they find that, largely, the tests confirm the results of their own assessments which they are required to record simultaneously.

The controversy will change in form, but will not diminish. In 1993, tests for 11-year-olds will fuel it further, while the league tables of schools' raw test results will mislead parents and fall like grapeshot among schools.

Two issues in particular have inflamed the controversy. One is the air of almost KGB-like secrecy which has dominated the test development process. The SEAC, unlike the NCC, has never come of age. Reports that are likely to be critical have been held back or even suppressed.

The other is the constant accusation that the SATs are necessary because they show that teachers' own assessments underestimate pupils' achievement. The charge was levelled first by the NFER, most notably by its director, Clare Burstall, in an article in *The Guardian* on the Tuesday after Easter in 1991. It was rapidly picked up by ministers anxious to justify their policy during the debacle of the SATs themselves. In fact, neither the NFER nor the Government have ever produced a shred of evidence for their view. Clare Burstall admitted this in correspondence with the NUT. What was revealed in 1991 was that in as many as a third of cases, SAT results were higher than teacher assessment results. There are a number of explanations for this, not least the fact that the children had had another term in which to progress. In any case, in some of the SATs it was demonstrably easier to record a given level than in the teacher assessment. In short, teachers may or may not underestimate pupils: SATs provide no evidence either way. This controversy is likely to die in 1992, because changed regulations allowed teachers to record teacher assessments and SATs at the same time rather than in different terms; even so, it has left a bitterness which will not dissipate so rapidly.

The Government has made clear its determination to insist on tests in England and Wales. It presented to the public the view that it must because teacher unions are resistant to change and utterly opposed to the testing parents want. In fact, the NUT and some other teacher organizations have proposed constructive alternatives to the present testing proposals, which have been supported by national organizations of governors and parents. These would make teacher assessment the main means of assessment. National standards would be ensured through moderation and validation organized by LEAs (or their successors) and through teachers using nationally-designed SATs from time to time to check their own assessments. Ironically, these proposals are very similar to those which the Government has published for the assessment of the core subjects in Scotland. Perhaps, as Dong McAvoy claimed in a published letter to John Patten in June 1992, the Government really does trust teachers in Scotland more. Whatever the truth, if the Government had more humility and less ideological baggage, there would be an opportunity for it to develop a consensus on curriculum and testing during 1993. The NUT's determination to provide an alternative set of testing proposals was evidence of a shift of direction in policy in 1990. The publication in April of that year of *A Strategy for the Curriculum* represented a new approach which went beyond response.

### Beyond Response

Given the Government's determination to ignore the profession, a union policy based on responding to Government proposals was clearly inadequate. The publication of *A Strategy for the Curriculum* and the alternative testing proposals some months later represented a new approach. A positive vision of the curriculum in the future was set out, the steps necessary to move towards it were explained and an attempt was made to campaign publicly for support. If the Government would not respond directly, it would be pressurised in the long run by the building up of a more effective alternative.

The curriculum vision of *A Strategy for the Curriculum* involved a National Curriculum of core skills, knowledge and understanding which would nevertheless leave space for a local level curriculum which in turn would leave space for a school and even classroom-level curriculum to be developed. It was a Russian doll model of the curriculum. A national core doll, enveloped successively by local and school dolls. It would be tested through moderated teacher assessment. As regards the publication of results, such a central element of the government's plans, the NUT document called for national discussions on:

> ... what an effective school is and how its effectiveness can be evaluated. This process should lead to parents and others receiving a much more accurate picture of schools than published test results can ever provide. (A strategy for the Curriculum para 4.30)

This call for national discussions on performance indicators has so far fallen on deaf ears, but was clarified and repeated in various NUT publications in the summer of 1992. It is a tragedy that the Government's ideological hostility to unions had blinded its ability to see the potential for consensus across the whole of curriculum, assessment and reporting. Yet the very success of models which government admires — in Germany for instance — depends precisely upon such social consensus about the goals of publicly provided education.

The NUT's success in building alliances for its curriculum and assessment proposals remains mixed. The high points were two joint deputations to ministers in 1991 with the NAHT and representatives of four national organizations of parents and governors. For the moment, however, the doors of Government remain firmly closed.

Other doors remain ajar. From the middle of 1990 onwards, relations between the teacher organizations and the NCC have steadily improved. There is much to be gained on both sides. The NCC depends ultimately for success on its reception among teachers (its customers, as David Pascall, its current chairman, calls them). Similarly, given the hostility of the Government and the sensitivity of SEAC, the NCC is the best available source of information and, ultimately, of influence.

The teacher organizations meet on a termly basis with the NCC and SEAC. Whatever divisions they may have over pay and conditions, they find it reasonably easy to agree a line on curriculum and assessment issues. The frustrations they have normally result from the political boundaries which, written or unwritten, limit the room for manoeuvre of the advisory bodies. There is little publicly available evidence of the extent to which, behind the scenes, NCC staff take up the views of teachers in their discussions with ministers. The replacement in rapid succession of Duncan Graham and Philip Halsey, the first Chairmen of the NCC and the SEAC, in the July coups of 1991 demonstrate, however, where the power ultimately lies. Each year, too, the Government replaces some members of each body. The tendency has been to shift both steadily to the right. While David Pascall, Duncan Graham's replacement at the NCC, has consistently claimed a degree of independence from the Government, Lord Griffiths at the SEAC remains distant from the profession and close to ministers. Winning hearts and minds does not appear to be on his agenda. The SEAC in turn limits the NCC's room for manoeuvre: indeed there is evidence that, behind the scenes, the NCC believes that there is a danger of assessment plans leading the curriculum. SEAC's advice on Key Stage 3 tests in 1991, for example, described the National Curriculum as 'a means of assessing pupil's progress and reporting it to parents'. Some of the pressure on the widely supported English National Curriculum results from the difficulty the SEAC perceives in designing means of testing it. Thus, although some doors are ajar, they are still difficult to squeeze through. And, once through, representatives of teachers find themselves only in the ante-chamber. The king's parlour remains bolted and activities behind the closed door a mystery. The teacher organizations have consistently pressed for NCC and SEAC to be merged. They will however draw little comfort from the Government's plans to combine them in the School Curriculum and Assessment Authority, since it is unlikely to be firmly in the grip of the Secretary of State.

While, therefore, influence at national level is strictly circumscribed at least in the short term, teachers, nevertheless, retain influence in the schools. It is they, after all, who implement the decisions as they emerge. The NUT President in 1990, June Fisher, recognized this in her inaugural speech, in which she urged teachers to stop 'whingeing' and 'win from within'. This was what teachers had done with TVEI. It is too early to say to what extent this is happening, but such research evidence as is available — supported by anecdotal evidence — reveals a profession of, ultimately, pragmatists making sense out of nonsense and providing as coherent a bill of fare for their pupils as is possible in a world where politicians have become as fickle and interfering as the Red Queen in Alice in Wonderland.

## Common Sense

Tom Paine opened his great work, *Common Sense*, with an expression of hope:

> . . . I offer nothing more than simple facts, plain arguments and common sense; and have no other preliminaries to settle with the reader, other than that he will divest himself of prejudice and prepossession . . .

Paine's eloquent call for common sense and an absence of prejudice is as close as one can come to the attitude of the teaching profession as a whole to the National Curriculum.

On the whole, in spite of the nonsense, teachers have grown to accept and even to like the National Curriculum. A survey of teacher opinion reported in the *TES* on 27 March 1992 showed that, of all Government reforms over recent years, the National Curriculum was the one they thought had done most to raise standards. Not only that, it is they who have made it work. All the evaluations of National Curriculum implementation pay tribute to the commitment and skill of teachers in implementing it. The same applies to evaluations of SATs incidentally, which, according to the same TES survey, less than one-fifth of teachers think have raised standards. This commitment to pupils, in spite of profound doubts about the nature of reform, is a hallmark of the teaching profession. The Government would do well to recognize it, for without it its programme would be in tatters.

Teachers' commitment to the National Curriculum should not be seen as unqualified support for all aspects of it. The evidence of the Leverhulme project at the University of Exeter is that between 1989 and 1991, teachers became no more, and in most cases less, confident about their ability to implement the National Curriculum in all subjects except science. This suggests on the one hand a continuing need for investment in training for the National Curriculum, and on the other a growing realization among teachers of the practical obstacles to progress as they became familiar with the National Curriculum as it is currently constructed.

Overall, teachers find themselves on the horns of a dilemma or two. They recognize a wide range of problems with the National Curriculum, though they like the general idea. They would like the problems — in particular the extent of prescription — ironed out; but ironing them out means more change, the idea of which, on top of all the other changes currently affecting them, they would rather do without. This dilemma faces policy-makers too. Proposals for solving this dilemma and reviewing the National Curriculum are contained in the programme in the final chapter of the book.

Meanwhile, teachers in schools across the land are continuing to implement and interpret the National Curriculum in their own schools. Apart from the sweeping and rather vague generalizations of HMI on the nature of this process, little evidence has emerged of what the reality of the National Curriculum in schools consists of in practice. This is not surprising given that the National Curriculum remains in the relatively early stages of implementation.

Perhaps the most important contribution so far to what will become a critical field of study is Richard Bowe's and Stephen Ball's book *Reforming Education and Changing Schools* (1992) Based on a series of interviews with teachers in four case study secondary schools, Bowe and Ball reached the parts of the implementation process that others have not yet reached. They discovered that the National Curriculum texts are being given very different interpretations in different schools. As one Head of Maths put it to the researchers:

> . . . my commitment is to the scheme we're using, and to make sure
> the National Curriculum is done within that but not to change the
> way we're working because of the National Curriculum. (p. 93)

A Head of English in a different school made a similar point:

> . . . we think our basic approach is correct . . . and that we're going to
> look at our approach and see where the National Curriculum and the
> profile components fit into our activities . . .

In short, Bowe and Ball conclude, if the Government reform circumscribes teachers' room for manoeuvre, it is also necessary to recognize 'the limits . . . practitioners place upon the State to reach into the daily life of schools' (p. 85).

Ultimately, therefore, the National Curriculum as experienced by pupils will be different in every school, a messy compromise which takes account of the school's policy, staffing and resources as well as the nationally-prescribed texts. Bill Lahr makes this point in his chapter. However much, therefore, the Government tries to exclude representatives of teachers from policy-making, teachers themselves will be a major influence on the outcome. For Government policy to succeed, it will need to take that reality into account.

## A Creative Relationship

Following a General Election and the appointment of a new Secretary of State for Education, there was a real opportunity to develop a creative relationship between the Government and teachers. It is a tragedy that so far instead of gasping the opportunity, John Patten has refused even to meet teacher representatives. The National Curriculum provides the ideal focus for rebuilding confidence between the two. In spite of doubts about the implementation process and aspects of its content, as we have seen, teachers recognize its potential to raise standards. There is, in addition, a national body, the NCC, which has won the confidence of the profession. The Government needs now to recognize the importance of a revision of the National Curriculum if it is to succeed in levering up standards. To do so, it will need to shut out the clamour of the ideologues on the right and listen instead to the pragmatic advice of those whose daily task it is to implement the National Curriculum. The extent to which the Government does so will be a good indicator of whether it is genuinely interested in raising standards across the country rather than driving through an ideological experiment of unknown consequences.

There is now a considerable body of research on the implementation of major reform in education. The best summary of it appears in Michael Fullan's seminal book *The New Meaning of Educational Change*, (Cassell, 1991). The National Curriculum, and the relationship between the Government and teachers upon which its success depends, would benefit if the lessons of that research are taken into account. It could provide a starting point for building that important creative relationship.

Lesson one provides the framework. Governments tend to take the view that change results from pressure on an inert system; teachers on the other hand argue it comes from the provision of support in the form of advice, training and material resources. The research shows that both are essential. The Schools' Council era gave us support without pressure. The last five years have seen pressure without support. The next five years ought to see both.

Lesson two follows logically. Those charged with implementation — teachers — need motivation. Successes should be celebrated, difficulties collaboratively solved and a vision of the future set out. With a government attitude based on suspicion, the policy would be doomed to failure.

Successful change requires substantial investment: this is the third clear lesson. The Coopers and Lybrand costings contained in John Atkins' chapter make a riveting read. If the Government rejects those findings, it should publish costs of its own. In any event, it would be unforgiveable with a reform of this magnitude for there to be no investment strategy. Nissan invested $30,000 per staff member in training and preparation before it opened its new plant in Tennessee in the mid-1980s. Successful change is expensive, in the public sector as well as the private sector. The cost of failure to invest is, however, much greater: the fact that it would be measured in the missed life chances of young people and economic failure in the next century is no excuse for discounting it.

The fourth lesson is predictable too. Training and professional development must be sustained through the implementation period. It is not sufficient to train people and leave them to it. There are two reasons why. Firstly, many of the problems and difficulties only emerge during implementation. It is then, as well as at the outset, that training is necessary. Secondly, unless the scheme is perfect, the implementation process will lead to the identification of design faults. The plan then needs to be changed with obvious consequences for training and development. In the case of the National Curriculum, this has happened with attainment targets in maths and science, with technology as a whole and with assessment at Key Stage 1. It will happen again.

Finally, no change as major as the National Curriculum will succeed in the long run unless it wins the hearts and minds of teachers. In a process like education where so much depends on the quality of relationships between teacher and teacher and, above all, teacher and pupil, successful change cannot be brought about through subjugation.

To misquote Tacitus, it does not make sense to make a wilderness and call it change. The NCC's 1991 Corporate Plan shows welcome recognition of the need to generate enthusiasm in the profession. There is evidence that in the case of the National Curriculum, if not other current reforms, teachers are indeed learning to love it. If it became evident to teachers that the Government saw them as partners in the creation of a curriculum that would empower every young person by the end of the century, their enthusiasm would know no bounds. A wise minister would now see the opportunity to unlock that fettered potential.

## References

BARBER, M. (1992) *Education and the Teacher Unions*, London, Cassell.
BOWE, R. and BALL, S.J. (1992) *Reforming Education and Changing Schools*, London, Routledge.
FULLAN, M. (1991) *The New Meaning of Educational Change*, London, Cassell.

*Chapter 3*

# Observations of an Outsider

*David Tytler*

Chroniclers of the curriculum come in a number of shapes and sizes, displaying equally varied degrees of cynicism. There is the elegance of *The Daily Telegraph*, the earnestness of *The Independent*, the erudition of *The Guardian*, and the misplaced enthusiasm of *The Daily Mail*. *The Times* remains aloof, having no truck with opting out or selection, but believing passionately that Britain's children should be given a full dose of geography.

Some of the education correspondents see themselves as professors of education and prefer to indulge in philosophical arguments with ministers and union officials, while others see themselves as the reporters they should be, anxious to find the story and tell it in a way that can be understood by their readers. And the years since 1987 have been rich in significant education stories, none more so than the introduction of the National Curriculum as part of the 1988 Education Reform Act.

The education correspondents and their newspapers generally welcomed the introduction of the National Curriculum but, as the reforms unfolded, so did a number of difficulties and apparent changes of direction as the education service had to cope with three Education Secretaries from 1989 to 1992, all having their own markedly different views of how the curriculum should be introduced into England's schools. (Wales had to contend with its own Secretary of State and separate Curriculum Council for Wales.)

Kenneth Baker, the self-styled father of the curriculum, was not necessarily liked, but his unfailing knack of producing a story every time he opened his mouth was much admired. An initiative a day meant a story a day, which made reporters and news editors alike happy men. Baker's genuine enthusiasm for the curriculum could not be doubted either.

So what a change when the likeable but reticent Scot, John MacGregor, moved into Elizabeth House, the ugly DES headquarters by Waterloo railway station which have now been deserted for the tree-filled, fountain-playing, glass-walled Sanctuary Buildings. A man who thought long and hard before making a decision — some officials believed too hard and too long — he was not an instant and regular supplier of the good quote.

Both Baker and MacGregor, however, had an easy relationship with journalists and generally seemed concerned about how they and the reforms were received. The amiable Kenneth Clarke made it clear on arrival that he did not care two hoots what journalists thought or wrote. He was going to do things his way come hell or high water, and professed an abhorrence of leaks. He once said: 'Don't think I am going to come to lunch with next week's press notice in my pocket'.

He was, however, a great man for the quote, often appearing to think aloud, as when he told a press briefing at the 1991 annual conference of the Secondary Heads Association (SHA) in Edinburgh that he often wondered why he did not do away with the Schools Examination and Assessment Council (SEAC) and the National Curriculum Council (NCC).

He was having a particularly difficult time with both bodies: he had not forgiven the NCC for stubbornly defending the National Curriculum for all children in state schools from 5 to 16 while the SEAC was attempting to provide acceptable Standard Assessment Tasks for Key Stage 3 which Mr Clarke described as elaborate nonsense. His general distrust of the SATs was summed up when he said: 'When I first looked at the papers I thought tasks was a typing mistake. They are tests aren't they?'

Sometimes it seemed as if the Government, its civil servants and advisers had lost sight of the fact that whatever they did or said would in the end affect many thousands of children in 25,000 schools, not to mention 400,000 teachers. MacGregor began the shift in attitude to his two quangos after considerable pressure that they were being taken over by the educational professionals and something should be done to stop them.

MacGregor had his chance in August 1990 when he was able to replace three retiring members of the NCC with two industrialists and the head of a grant-maintained school. One of the industrialists was David Pascall, of BP, and a former member of Mrs Thatcher's Downing Street think tank. A year later he went on to be appointed part-time Chairman of the NCC when Duncan Graham resigned as Chairman and Chief Executive.

Having delivered the curriculum on time, the Council now found itself increasingly under attack for over-prescription and over-complexity while all it had been doing was to carry out the requirements of the 1988 Act. The difficulties were inevitable once it had been decided that the curriculum was to be introduced subject by subject.

The first official unveiling of the details of the National Curriculum came in the unprepossessing setting of the Notting Hill Gate headquarters of SEAC where the fledgling NCC was an unwilling temporary lodger before moving off to its new riverside headquarters in York.

Maths and science were the first of the ten subjects to be released on a suspicious world peopled by unhappy teachers and cynical journalists. The framework for the compulsory National Curriculum had been set out by Kenneth Baker in GERBIL, the Government's Education Reform Bill, but nobody was entirely sure what the subject working parties would come up with after their crash delivery programmes.

The early months of the mathematics working party had been an unmitigated disaster for the Government, and at times it must have looked to Baker as if the antics of the group were threatening the very existence of the National Curriculum, which was designed to bring rigour and improved standards for all young people aged 5 to 16 in maintained schools in England and Wales.

The group had been riven by internal division which had been widely reported in the national newspapers. The debate hinged on the use of calculators and whether or not children should be taught how to do long division. The interim report had been savaged by Baker and its Chair replaced with Duncan Graham, the former Chief Education Officer of Suffolk, and at that time the Chief Executive of Humberside County Council.

Graham announced the final reports of the maths and science working groups on 16 August 1988, sixteen days after the 1988 Education Reform Act had come into force. On the same day, it was also announced that he had been appointed Chair and Chief Executive of the newly-created National Curriculum Council.

The education correspondents who crowded into that small room in Notting Hill Gate wanted to know only one thing: had the working party delivered the return to traditional standards that Baker had so publicly demanded. The answer, as in most of the subjects that were to follow, was a compromise. Children would be able to use calculators, but they must be able to show that they could understand the arithmetical process of long division and should learn their times tables.

In their excitement, the journalists failed to notice that the science working party had stolen earth sciences from the geographers. But science was to have its day with the public debate over the single and dual award science courses and the relative merits of the three sciences and the balanced science course proposed by the working party and endorsed by the NCC.

MacGregor, whose own children had been educated in independent secondary schools, seemed to pay undue attention to the demands of the independent school heads, particularly those in the Headmasters' Conference and the Girls' Schools Association, even though they could pick and choose what they wanted out of the National Curriculum, unlike the state schools who were compelled to follow it.

The SEAC had recommended in March 1990 that GCSE science should be taken as a comprehensive balanced science course, carrying two passes or a single award examination based on an equally tough but shorter course. Single sciences could only be taken at 'A' level by students who had gained the GCSE double award. The independent schools, at the behest of HMC, fought a rearguard action to protect their traditional science lessons and won.

Whether it was a significant victory remains to be seen. Very few state schools will choose the option, if only because pupils would have to take all three sciences if they were to meet the requirements of the National Curriculum. It is also very doubtful that all pupils, even in a majority of independent boys' schools ever did all three.

As the subjects unfolded, the final reports of the working party were usually launched at a press briefing attended by Duncan Graham or one of his senior officers, but the November 1988 report of the English working party, which had suffered similar trials and tribulations to their colleagues in the maths group, was presented by a senior civil servant who could not be quoted or named.

She made it clear, however, that the Secretary of State, Kenneth Baker, was unhappy with the report for 5 to 11-year-olds and thought that it was 'too woolly', her very words, when it came to the teaching of grammar. The NCC duly tightened things up, much to the annoyance of the working party, which was still considering the secondary curriculum. Whether there was enough tightening is a matter of opinion!

When the final English orders were laid before Parliament in March 1989, Kenneth Baker, lover of poetry and Secretary of State for Education, insisted that all primary school children should learn some poetry by heart, a benign intervention, but the first clear indication that the National Curriculum was subject to political whim.

The biggest intervention was over history, which had troubled all three Education Secretaries and was the best example of the debate over facts versus judgment. The Government favoured facts, which the history working party accepted were vital to the understanding of history, but could not be judged separately. Which facts were to be tested?

It eventually fell to Clarke to decide. And he did. He ruled that in both history and geography the emphasis should be on facts rather than opinion. He did go some way to meeting critics who had complained about his original decision that modern history teaching should cover only the period from the turn of the century to the 1960s. Modern history now ends twenty years ago, with the cut-off point moving forward in five-year intervals. It is reasonable to ask whether the nation should have a compulsory curriculum that is so vulnerable to the whims of ministers and what safeguards there are. One would be a fiercely independent National Curriculum Council, which at the moment is eluding us.

The first public rumblings that all was not well with the National Curriculum at Key Stage 4 for 14 to 16-year-olds surfaced in Novermber 1989. Once again, it was the independent schools which made the running, even though they were not compelled to follow the curriculum, although in practice most of them do. Headmistresses at the annual conference of the Girls' School Association in Harrogate complained that the conflict surrounding the GCSE and attainment targets for 16-year-olds were preventing them from planning their curriculum properly.

The problem was that if the full National Curriculum course was combined with GCSEs there would barely be room to cover the ten compulsory subjects, let alone introduce subjects outside the compulsory curriculum, such as a second modern language, the classics or economics. Schools that wanted to add other subjects would be faced with logistically insuperable problems.

Angela Rumbold, the Minister of State, shared the heads' concerns. A story was leaked to *The Times* which indicated Rumbold's thinking at the end of 1989. The Government was considering making some subjects in the National Curriculum optional, cutting back on others and bypassing GCSE courses for 14 to 16-year-olds. An anonymous minister told *The Times*: 'It is quite apparent that at 14 something is going to have to give for some children.'

The first suggestion of the extended core appeared with the Government indicating that all children up to 16 would have to study maths, English and science and that a modern language and technology might also be added to the list. The first indication that all ten National Curriculum subjects were not after all going to be compulsory came in January when MacGregor addressed the annual meeting of the Society of Education Officers.

He said that some pupils would be able to drop certain subjects, that new GCSEs would be introduced in combined subjects and that half-GCSEs might be taught in others. All pupils would have to take full GCSE courses in maths, science and English and would continue to study technology and a modern language until they were 16.

Schools would be able to provide courses in the other subjects which did not come up to full GCSE standards, but which would meet National Curriculum requirements. MacGregor also said that he was considering making PE optional as he believed that this could largely be achieved in after-school activities. Again, he was falling prey to the notion that state schools could follow the independent example where sports were often provided outside normal school hours. Like too many Conservative ministers, MacGregor has little idea of what actually happens in the state schools for which they are responsible.

The NCC's final suggestion in November 1990 was that the extended core should take 60 per cent of the timetable, with 10 per cent divided between history or geography, either as combined subjects or as single subjects, 10 per cent to art, music and PE, to be divided the way the school decided, 5 per cent to religious, personal and social education, which would leave 15 per cent for other subjects.

Whether or not this would have been acceptable to MacGregor will never be known as he was replaced by Kenneth Clarke following Geoffrey Howe's resignation. It was not acceptable to Clarke. Within a few days of taking over as Education Secretary, Clarke told *The Times*: 'It is not instantly apparent that they (the NCC) have taken in what has been said. The curriculum must not become prescriptive and exclude the whole variety of options that people want to exercise.'

Clarke certainly exercised his options. At the North of England education conference a year after MacGregor had raised the question of Key Stage 4, Clarke rejected the advice of the Council. Children would be required to take only maths, science and English at GCSE. All pupils from the age 11 to 16 would also have to take courses in a modern language and technology, but not necessarily to GCSE.

From 14, children would have to take either history or geography or a course combining both. Music and art would be optional, but all children would be expected to take some sort of physical exercise which could range from organized sport to aerobics.

Clarke changed the face of the National Curriculum. As reluctant to leave health as MacGregor was to leave education, Clarke saw his brief as to unravel much of what had been done before him. Always charming, it was as if inside a nice man was a nasty man trying to get out. He offended many within the education service where MacGregor had always listened patiently. Clarke knew there was little time for courtesy and consideration. He was a man in a hurry who severely altered the National Curriculum as originally envisaged, while destroying Her Majesty's Inspectors of Schools along the way. He has had his reward in the Conservative election victory and now holds one of the great offices of state. Where this has left the country's state schools remains to be seen.

*Part 2*

*Perspectives from the School*

# Chapter 4

# The National Curriculum in
# a Primary School

*Anne Waterhouse*

There has, indeed, been a great deal of sense and nonsense expounded about the National Curriculum since July 1987 when the Government published the National Curriculum 5–16 consultation document, with the rationale that 'a National Curriculum backed by clear assessment arrangements will help to raise standards of attainment' (DES/Welsh Office, 1987). There is also an ironic significance in the former Chairman of the National Curriculum Council and an official of the largest, and most critical, teachers' union jointly editing this response to the statutory curriculum requirements of the 1988 Education Reform Act. Such an alliance, unimaginable in the immediate post-implementation days, reflects inherent paradoxes within the Act itself, and the conflict between the competitive philosophies of the market place and equality of opportunity for all children to achieve to their level of potential within the structures of an entitlement curriculum.

I trained as an infant teacher in the late 1960s and began work through the early days of the Plowden era. I have always considered myself to be 'child-centred'. After all, what are schools for if not to work with children? At the same time, however, I also subscribe to the view that there should be a National Curriculum, with decisions about what children learn being made by the wider community. The responsibility for how this should be presented to the children should, however, rest with teachers and schools following consultations with parents, governors and appropriate representatives from the community.

By the beginning of the 1992/93 school year, the statutory framework laid down in the 1988 Education Reform Act was in place. Each of the National Curriculum subject orders is complete. Its complexities are beyond anything I had previously envisaged. I think it is appropriate for children to experience as wide a range of opportunities across the spectrum of human knowledge as possible. As this knowledge has increased it has been organized into subject disciplines to enable sense to be made of what otherwise would be unmanageable. Despite my child-centred upbringing, I believe that children need to learn about the specific qualities of separate subjects. The manner in which these subjects are constructed into a whole curriculum should enable children to make sense of separate subjects and should provide real opportunities for putting skills into practice. In other words, an integrated curriculum should contain essential skills and subject knowledge structured to enable progression and continuity for all children.

There is, however, a wide difference between providing children with their entitlement to access to a wide range of knowledge, and forcing them to learn facts and information in isolation from the experiences and meanings of their lives. Whilst I would not argue with the need to ensure that children receive knowledge in an ordered and structured way, I cannot accept the growing view that to teach these subjects in isolation is the best and only way forward to raise standards of learning and performance throughout post-ERA schooling. The current debate about the delivery of the National Curriculum to the children in our schools is based on a narrow and simplistic view that the curriculum on offer should rest almost entirely upon knowledge, with the skills, attitudes and confidence necessary to access this information considered as unimportant.

I believe that children have to be taught from the outset the necessary skills to enable them to learn. Although I dispute that standards are falling, there is no doubt that they are changing. Reception children are entering our schools with a very different range of skills and knowledge from their peers twenty years ago. Four and 5-year-old children today are generally extremely adept at the mysteries of the video recorder and arcade-type computer games and are extremely aware about the tensions of adult life as portrayed through television soap operas.

Many reception children do not have sufficient manual dexterity or hand-eye coordination necessary to develop the fine motor skills which underpin reading and writing skills. Convenience foods and the pace of modern life very often preclude the former pre-school experience gained from, for example, rolling pastry dough and cutting out and sticking, when children joined with their parents undertaking the necessities of domestic life. Infant-aged children today are extremely knowledgeable but generally unable to deal with basic decision-making, turn-taking, social relationships — they lack independence skills. These same children are, however, expected to make sense of National Curriculum technology, for example, and 'identify needs and opportunities' or 'generate a design' when they are lacking the basic human experiences necessary to make sense of the prescribed statutory requirements. Christine's mum came to see me very concerned because her year 2 daughter was upset and having disturbed nights over a 'bird scarer' which would not work out properly. 'Why can't the teacher just tell the children what to do instead of making them waste time trying things out?' Mum was not over-impressed with the technology Programme of Study or relevant Attainment Targets.

The paradox of the National Curriculum is apparent within the generally accepted sense of structuring knowledge to enable children to make better sense of their lives and the world in which they live, whilst at the same time removing some of the flexibility for harnessing natural inquisitiveness and the learning of skills necessary for the development of 'whole' people. For children to learn and to progress towards the perceived 'holy grail' of higher standards, account has to be taken of how they learn and what provides the motivation to learn and to achieve. The nonsense of the National Curriculum, as it stands, is that it takes little or no account of how children learn. The current political debate is also generating its own nonsensical dogma relating to the perform-ance of children, teachers and styles of teaching and school organization.

From the perspective of a small primary school, or indeed any school, the implementation of the National Curriculum cannot be divorced from the effects of the other major areas of enforced change embodied within the Edu-cation Reform Act itself. Local Management of Schools (LMS) and the con-sequences of formula funding are beginning to impact upon all levels of organization and resourcing. The twin issues of open enrolment and opting out, with the use of competition between schools as a strategy to raise standards, have barely surfaced. The enforced publication of confusing and misleading comparative statistical results will do little or nothing to ease these problems and the confusion between parental choice and parental preference. It is also a nonsense to impose reporting regulations upon schools, such as those which arrived in May 1992 and expect the consequential tensions between parents and schools to be resolved through explanatory Department for Education leaflets.

Parental expectations and public preconceptions and misconceptions, informed by such bland and misleading Government information leaflets and endless Charters, cause problems for schools. If small schools fail to compete they will inevitably become unviable because of the financial constraints of LMS. Competition has a negative effect on professional development and the sharing of ideas and learning experiences with colleagues in other schools. There has been an undoubtedly detrimental effect on cooperative cluster arrangements in our area. Colleagues from neighbouring schools are wary of sharing good practice because of the tensions of competing for pupils and the anxieties now developing over pressures from some governing bodies to consider seeking grant maintained status. There are consequential implications and anxieties for the success of headteacher appraisal. It is going to be very difficult to welcome a visiting headteacher colleague into school for the purposes of appraisal when that same colleague could be competing for the same 'age-weighted pupil units', otherwise known as children! We are fortu-nate in that our LEA is sympathetic to this anxiety and is structuring the scheme across neighbouring districts rather than local schools.

Given the prevailing political climate, the expected pressures on schools to leave local authority control is likely to have a domino effect. I am strongly opposed to this unnecessary extension of the market philosophy because I believe that it will exacerbate the problems caused by current funding arrangements which already lead to gross inequalities with larger schools benefiting on the basis of economy of scale. Our school is too small to reap any long-term benefits from opting out. To attempt to increase its size drastically would risk destroying the ethos which teachers, children, governors and parents have worked so hard to develop over the years. The process of competition, including the publication of National Curriculum results, could cause successful schools to change those elements which are the precise reasons for their success.

At a time when the demands of the National Curriculum are requiring more structured teaching at differentiated levels, our class sizes are increasing and look likely to be above thirty in the next school year. This is as a direct result of the forced staffing adjustments due to formula funding. In a school with five classes to cover the seven years of compulsory schooling, there has to be mixed age teaching. In particular, where there is an additional commitment to integrate children with statemented special educational needs, it is impossible to group children in age or ability classes. Regardless of any demands to class teach specific age groups, of necessity we have to consider alternative organizations for successful teaching and learning. More teaching time is being spent on administrative tasks as statutory requirements place more pressure on the clerical assistant, who is, of course, part-time in a small school. Many of her previous duties have to be undertaken by teachers. Although the parents at our school are incredibly supportive and are willing to undertake all sorts of voluntary duties to help, I feel very uneasy at the thought of seeking such assistance to manage the administration of the school. It is also extremely difficult to undertake much in terms of forward planning while the technicalities of the local authority's scheme for local management are subject to the changing whims of the Secretary of State.

The implementation of the National Curriculum has been affected by all of the ERA developments and itself has an effect on the ethos and values of the school. The prescriptive subject structures and assessment procedures imposed by the National Curriculum do not, on their own, guarantee children a worthwhile curriculum. All members of our school community are encouraged to view the school as a place for learning. Everyone works hard to promote and develop the spirit of partnership and pride in self-achievement. There are specific aims for children, teachers and parents, all incorporating Lawton's 'rights' of the child, which are:

    (i)    to have the respect of their teachers;
   (ii)    to have a worthwhile curriculum;
  (iii)    not to have their time wasted unnecessarily;
  (iv)    to be treated fairly;
   (v)    to be members of a community with an adequate rule system;
  (vi)    to complain;
 (vii)    to choose some activities; and
(viii)    to participate in some aspects of decision-making.
          (Lawton, 1981, p. 129)

Children do not progress on the basis of testing and recording alone. However, without clear assessment strategies, teachers cannot make decisions about the appropriate next stages of learning for their pupils. One of the sensible notions underpinning the National Curriculum has been the provision of a structured framework against which the progress of children can be planned and reported. After all, no builder builds a house without plans, usually drawn up by an architect. Individual teachers should not have the total responsibility for selecting what to teach, but I will defend to the last barricade the right for teachers through their professionalism to decide how to teach and structure learning experiences offered to their pupils. I also believe that parents should know what to expect their child to be learning and should have more detailed information about progress. Children in different parts of the country should have access to the same opportunities and should not be disadvantaged by where they live and attend school.

As well as the nonsense of the over-prescriptive nature of the present National Curriculum, the notion of entitlement for all has a hollow ring when not all schools are required to follow it. If this National Curriculum is going to be the saving grace for the future economic prosperity of the country then it is a nonsense for private education and City Technology Colleges to be exempt. It is also a nonsense that this so-called National Curriculum is not national. There are significant differences between learning experiences offered to children in England, Wales, Northern Ireland and Scotland with separate Curriculum Councils in England and Wales.

The former Chief Inspector of Schools expressed concern, in one of his annual reports, that some aspects of an over-prescriptive curriculum would undermine and deskill teachers' job satisfaction and morale. Teachers at our school have had to address these issues and consider many others affecting teaching and the organization of learning strategies for our children. We believe that where teachers are also learners, then they are enabled to be better teachers.

The National Curriculum in its present form places considerable pressures on available time. As a staff we are having to consider and reorder priorities to enable us to provide with the necessary learning support time for teachers to fulfil their other statutory duties. If teachers are unable to spend time together to evaluate and plan, then the quality of what is on offer to the children is inevitably reduced. The budgetary constraints of LMS do not make this juggling of time easy. Class and support teachers are also stressed by tensions between providing the best for their children and this time needed to plan and organize. Currently, our governors are involved with statutory consultations with parents to change times of the school day, partly as a consequence of an insufficient budget allocation to provide adequate lunchtime supervision and partly to reorganise teachers' directed time to make maximum use of time allocated to the children. There is also an increasing problem in enabling teachers to get out of school at the end of the day to attend twilight in-serice sessions because of changes to the GEST (Grants for Education Support and

Training) budget restricting the availability of courses and the ability of teachers to have access to them. In consequence, much of this training takes place at the end of a school day. Teachers are inevitably tired, and this growing exhaustion is taking its toll in increased stress-related absences. If National Curriculum training is so important, teachers should not be expected to attend in what amounts to their spare time.

The difficulties in enabling teachers to benefit from in-service training are reflected in their insecurity as they are expected to deal with unfamiliar subject areas of the new National Curriculum structures. It is particularly interesting to observe the performance of a newly-trained colleague, who has never experienced life in school without the National Curriculum, in comparison with experienced colleagues. All of us are struggling to provide a differentiated curriculum covering all the attainment targets and statements of attainment. Our newly-qualified colleague is better able to plan for differentiation by task. Experienced teachers tend to look for differentiation by outcome. The probationer is obviously not as competent in the width of subject experiences, or in classroom control and management, as his/her experienced colleagues but does not appear to be suffering the same traumas in adjusting to a more constrained curriculum.

These pressures upon teachers are having an inevitable consequence upon their self-confidence. A professional development model of appraisal should help in this area, but in a climate where payment by results is a very real possibility, such developments seem doomed to failure. In our school we have a relatively sophisticated programme of staff development. Colleagues are encouraged to record their own self-evaluations and express their views about their performance and the management and organization of the school in general. These views are then compiled anonymously for the identification of priorities for the school development plan. From initial scepticism about the advantages of school development planning, I have revised my views. I now see development planning as a means of protecting my colleagues, and the school, from constant externally imposed changes.

The National Curriculum structures take little or no account of how children learn or of the relevance of curriculum expectations for their motivation. To quote the old saying, 'you can lead a horse to water, but you can't make it drink'. The same applies to young children. There is a world of difference in providing children with their entitlement to learn the skills necessary to make sense of the world and presenting them with a fragmented curriculum consisting mainly of what, to them, are irrelevant facts. The National Curriculum Council attempted to resolve this problem by promoting health education, education for citizenship and the other cross-curricular themes and dimensions. Unfortunately, rigid subject structures of statutory attainment targets have, in many cases, led to these additional themes being viewed as bolt-ons and separate subjects in themselves.

Equality of opportunity and access to the whole curriculum is a major area of anxiety in our school. Over the years the staff have worked incredibly hard to ensure that all children are able to attempt the full range of curriculum experiences on offer. The school has developed the view that where children have a disability, the responsibility to ensure each child has appropriate learning experiences rests with the teacher. It is not the child who is the problem, but the teacher who *has* the problem. The majority of children who display unacceptable behaviour do so in the context of inappropriate expectations. We therefore try to differentiate the curriculum appropriately. No one is disapplied or has had the National Curriculum modified, because we believe that once we say to a child 'you are deaf so you can't be expected to listen' and disapply them from all the listening components of the curriculum, then that child has lost its equality of opportunity. With increasing pressures on schools to publish results, I feel a great sense of anxiety that we may be forced to reconsider this view to avoid the school as a whole presenting depressed results leading to our genuine 'success' being misrepresented as 'failure'.

The piecemeal introduction of the National Curriculum subject Orders has made it very difficult to plan. There is no doubt that science and mathematics currently dominate the curriculum as these were the first subjects which we had to assimilate. Criticisms from the inspectorate in relation to curriculum balance are probably correct. In our school there is no doubt that the aesthetic area of the curriculum declined while all our energies were concentrated upon developing our familiarity with individual subject Orders. There are also difficulties in relation to planning and delivery where the structures of the subjects are not the same. History is the classic example and is proving very difficult for us to cover within our existing patterns of thematic teaching and mixed age class orientation. The final three subjects; art, music and PE have different structures and the revision of the attainment targets for maths and science are causing us to review our ways of working yet again.

While I firmly believe that it is a vital part of a teacher's role to constantly review and assess, I am very concerned that we are not being given time to familiarize ourselves with National Curriculum Orders and are having to review and introduce different components at the same time as we are becoming more accountable and having to publish our results. All this is taking place in a growing climate of mistrust. The Standard Assessments Tasks during the summer of 1991 were supposed to be 'an unreported run'. Not only were these results widely published, but they have been misused to illustrate a supposed decline in standards. The results of the next run of Standard Assessment Tasks will be used in comparison, but again this will lead to misleading information as the assessments have been restructured and are not the same.

Despite all these reservations, the introduction of the National Curriculum, within the framework of the Education Reform Act, is not all negative. The National Curriculum and its more systematic assessment structures have helped us to look much more carefully at how we teach and how children learn. Parents are now able to compare the progress of their child against predetermined levels. We are providing children with a more structured curriculum, this is consistently presented throughout the school, offering clear lines of progression enabling children to work more closely to their level of potential.

One of the advantages of being a small school is that children are more able to work at their level, not solely in an age-related class. Following the findings of the effective schools research, we have attempted to offer a more focussed, 'blocked' timetable. For maths and language work, particularly at Key Stage 1, children tend to move to where a teacher is offering work at their appropriate level rather than have three teachers all trying to do the same thing. This is enabling us to make more efficient use of teaching and learning time. As indicated by the evaluations of National Curriculum implementations to date, there are difficulties at Key Stage 2, particularly in the subject knowledge required for the teachers of years 5 and 6.

The National Curriculum has enabled us to develop more coherent planning, assessing, recording and reporting procedures. The children and their parents are contributors to the recording and reporting. In the summer of 1991, the school presented written reports to parents for the first time. The report form was designed to belong to the child, following the principles of records of achievement. The children were responsible for writing their own self-evaluations so that parents were able to compare these with the comments of the teachers. Each child also has an ongoing developmental profile to which the parents have access at any time during the school year. There is a weekly consultation session (we call them 'surgeries') built into teacher's directed time, and parents know that they can call in at this time to talk to the teachers, read and contribute to the profiles. We also encourage parents to make appointments to come in and talk to us at other times if there are concerns or problems. The school invests a great deal of time working with and reporting to parents. Generally this has enabled a good basis of trust between home and school to develop, with obvious benefits for the quality of the educational experiences offered to the children.

What we need now is time. Time to consolidate and time to adjust to the major changes which have impacted upon schools over the past five years. There is no doubt in my mind that the critics of primary education are right when they say that teacher expectation and classroom organization are key factors in the levels of pupil achievement. For the National Curriculum to make sense, there needs to be a rationalization of expectations at all levels from central Government to children themselves, The rhetoric of the 'back to basics' movement needs to be redirected, to enable proper consultations with all interested parties, to determine what the National Curriculum should cover and how it should be presented.

This present National Curriculum model is over-prescriptive and places too many pressures on young children and their teachers. What the present debate and political dogma fail to address is that until primary schools are able to concentrate their attention on teaching young children how to learn instead of an over-emphasis on facts and content, then levels of pupil attainment will not rise. A National Curriculum should be a whole curriculum based on entitlement and access to balanced teaching and learning. We do not want a watered down version of the present National Curriculum, but a set of realistic and achievable expectations to enable every child, in every kind of school, to experience their entitlement to education for life. Schools also need the resources to enable them to work flexibly, teaching children in realistically-sized classes with appropriate equipment and in a safe, clean and healthy working environment. There has been a great deal of nonsense expounded about dogma and polarized points of view. What is needed now is for common sense to replace emotive responses and a re-examination of the purposes and values of primary education — please!

## References

DES/WELSH OFFICE (1987) *The National Curriculum 5–16: A Consultation Document*, London, HMSO.
LAWTON, D. (1981) *An Introduction to Teaching and Learning*, London, Hodder & Stoughton.

Chapter 5

# Equal Opportunities and the National Curriculum

*Elaine Foster and Anne-Marie Bathmaker*

### ERA: Circulars, Guidance and Equal Opportunities

The only piece of legislation which clearly indicates the premise upon which equal opportunities issues in the National Curriculum could be built is found in the opening section of the 1988 Education Reform Act:

> The curriculum of a school satisfies the requirements of the Act if it is a balanced and broadly-based curriculum which:
>
> (a) promotes the spiritual, moral, cultural, mental and physical development of pupils at the schools and of society: and
> (b) prepares such pupils for the opportunities, responsibilities and experiences of adult life.

Subsequent documents, with no statutory force, from the Department for Education and the National Curriculum Council provide us with interpretations and illustrations of the above aims of the Act:

> (The intention of the Act is to) reflect the culturally diverse society to which pupils belong and of which they will become adult members.

and, further:

> to prepare a pupil for his/her responsibilities as a citizen towards the community and society, nationally and internationally. (DES *Circular 5/89*, para 17)

> The foundation subjects are certainly not a complete curriculum . . . more will, however, be needed to secure the kind of curriculum required by section of the ERA . . . The whole curriculum for all pupils will certainly need to include as appropriate (and in some cases

all) stages ... coverage across the curriculum of gender and multi-cultural issues. (DES (1989) para 3.8)

In *Curriculum Guidance 3: The Whole Curriculum*, published by the NCC in 1990, equal opportunities 'for all pupils' is defined as follows:

> Equal opportunities is about helping all children to fulfil their potential. Teachers are rightly concerned when their pupils underachieve and are aware that educational outcomes may be influenced by factors outside the school's control such as a pupil's sex or social, cultural or linguistic background.

The document also suggests how schools might go about validating and securing the issues within the parameters of the whole curriculum:

> ... a commitment to providing equal opportunities for all pupils, and a recognition that preparation for life in a multicultural society is relevant to all pupils, should permeate every aspect of the curriculum ... schools need to foster a climate in which equality of opportunity is supported by a policy to which the whole school subscribes and in which positive attitudes to cultural diversity are actively promoted. (*ibid*, pp. 2–3)

Equal opportunities is described as a dimension: something which 'should permeate the whole curriculum'. Some have argued that this term itself is well suited as a misnomer for a watered-down approach to equal opportunities.

Overwhelmingly (in the above circulars, newsletters, pamphlets), there is an assumption of a shared understanding of the kind of equal opportunities education models that are being promoted. With no attempt at a detailed working definition, there appears to be scope for individual institutions to define, agree and publish their own brand of such policies. These emerged in patches across the country, and were significantly variable in their definition and aim.

Educationists have identified four models of educational response to ethnic minority pupils. These are: the assimilationist; the integrationist: cultural pluralism/diversity: and anti-racist. The models appear to be successive and clearly identifiable. However, as Bruce Gill (1991) points out:

> The phases do not mark neat transitions in thinking across the whole population: rather they refer to stages in thinking in the area of race policy. (p. 13)

The 1905s/60s assimilationist model was based on the thinking that immigrant pupils had language problems and marked religious and cultural differences, and that if these problems and differences could be 'remediated or removed', then 'they could be merged into mainstream society' whilst at the same time disruption to the education of indigenous children would be minimal.

By the late 1960s and into the mid-70s, a shift to integrationist thinking occurred. This sought to given recognition to ethnic minority pupils, languages, cultures and religions. Teachers were encouraged to become aware of the background of pupils and, where possible, to use this knowledge to inform their teaching. The presence of ethnic minority pupils in schools was, however, seen as contributing to the lowering of educational standards.

The aims of cultural pluralism included a greater understanding and recognition of, and respect for, ethnic minority cultures. The particular needs of ethnic minority pupils were to be met and all pupils to be prepared for life in a multiracial society.

The final phase, anti-racism, sought to ensure that education responded to the need for social and racial justice with an emphasis primarily on equality. Anti-racist education should challenge and counter racism, both within schools and beyond in the wider society. It should also tackle institutional as well as individual racism.

Nikki Fonda's typology describing gender equality is similarly useful in describing four approaches:

> ... the 'unlocked door', the 'open door', the 'special escalator' and 'equal outcomes'. The 'unlocked door' ensures that there are no formal barriers to girls, 'the open door' aims in addition to remove bias in teaching approach and content. The 'special escalator' provides compensatory provision and works to counteract stereotypes, and the 'equal outcomes' model seeks comparable achievement of boys and girls and similar outcomes in education and employment. (Fonda, 1989)

The development of educational policies which responded to the need for equal opportunities work was made possible through substantial central Government funds in the form of Section 11 and Educational Support Grants (ESG) for race, and the later Technical and Vocational Education Initiative (TVEI) for gender work.

Since April 1992, Section 11 funds are no longer available for work in this area and GEST and TVEI funds are winding down. The effects on equal opportunities education developments of Local Management of Schools (LMS) are yet to be assessed.

The lack of Section 11 or GEST funds has immediately removed personnel and material resources from schools. Schools that are operating under tight budgets are looking to lose staff, especially those who are not engaged in teaching a National Curriculum subject. The most effective model of developing equal opportunities education in schools depended upon the availability of senior staff who did not carry a large teaching timetable, but who could be engaged in team-teaching and professional development courses alongside staff in classrooms or across departments. These developments were supported, and often promoted, by LEA advisory and inspectorial staff.

The proactive role of the LEA has been largely substituted by a role which is reactive to schools' demands. With LMS there is a very real fear that many posts dedicated to equal opportunities will be lost. The pressing need from many schools' points of view is to squeeze the content of the National Curriculum into the available time, and to train staff to teach the content, and to introduce and administer the Standard Assessment Tasks (SATs).

## National Curriculum Subjects, Themes and Dimensions

Advice on equal opportunities in the National Curriculum is to be found in the supplementary guidance to the chairs of the subject working groups. This was issued by the Secretary of State for Education, as amplification of certain aspects of the National Curriculum which the groups needed to bear in mind in their deliberations. It stated:

> It will also be important to bear in mind that the curriculum should provide equal opportunities for boys and girls . . . you should also take account of the school population and society at large.

This was obviously broad enough for there to be a number of responses drawn from various models of equal opportunities and multicultural education.

In the main, the working groups chose to dwell on the following issues: opportunities or the lack of them for boys and girls and for pupils from ethnic minority groups to fully participate in a particular subject area; and how teachers could teach a curriculum which reflected the contributions of an ethnic-ally diverse school or society.

The working groups identified a number of obstacles to equality of opportunity for girls and boys. Broadly speaking, these fall into the following categories:

(i) expectations and attitudes of teachers to girls' and boys' perform-ance in subject areas;

(ii) curriculum content differentiated in terms of gender: for example, girls taking biology (seen as a soft option) and boys being taught competitive sports such as football;

(iii) the use of language and subject content which does not recognise women's contributions; and

(iv) the low expectations, attitudes and responses of girls and boys to certain subjects.

The working groups also highlighted examples of good practice which teachers and schools could put in place. Teachers, they suggested, should have high expectations of their pupils:

It has often been reported that one of the consistent characteristics of successful language teaching is that the teacher has, and is able to communicate, high expectations clearly and positively to the pupils. (MFL 14.11)

Teachers should also be able to challenge their own, pupils' and others' stereotyping, language and subject content:

A study of the subject matter of art can also contribute significantly to helping pupils challenge traditional attitudes towards gender issues. (Art)

In order to ensure that boys and girls are equally motivated by what they are studying, relevant material which recognizes women's and men's achievements and contributions should be selected and presented to pupils. Again the art working group suggested:

One approach to this is to present pupils with examples of work of artists, crafts workers, and designers of both sexes ...

The history working group clarifies why it adopted this no nonsense approach in the following terms:

Our approach is intended to combat inherited stereotypes. Women should be studied not only as part of social history (where it is still assumed they 'belong') but in contexts often treated as exclusively male, such as politics, war, commerce and science.

A few of the working groups adopted a 'blaming the victim' tone when they talked of the expectations and attitudes of girls or boys to aspects of subjects which appear to favour/encourage boys or girls. For example, in music:

On the other hand, microtechnology and pop music appear to have attracted more boys to GCSE since it began — a welcome trend, provided that it does not conceal a disinclination on the part of girls towards that area of musical experience. (Music 11.9)

There appears to be very little analysis in the 5–16 documents of the different ways in which sexism affects men and women. To present materials about women's contributions or involvement in a particular area of study might not in itself serve to challenge stereotyped notions of women. The presentation which starts with what men did, but ends with 'but of course there was a woman' will mainly perpetuate men's position without affecting the core issue of sexism.

Although recognition of women's work and their contributions and the introduction of anti-sexist language might be a valuable starting point, teachers and schools cannot be 'smug' in thinking that this is equal opportunities permeating the National Curriculum. The existing ideologies and systems which have served to invalidate women's experiences cannot be left unchallenged.

Black women/girls often experience both racism and sexism. The working groups generally failed in their deliberations to link these. Only the PE working group goes some way towards making the connection:

> Teachers should be sensitive to the biological and cultural effects of being female or male, on the behaviour considered 'appropriate' for girls and boys of different cultures. (PE para. 30)

Many of the categories of responses to gender inequalities are common to ethnic diversity. However, there are peculiarities. Unlike gender issues, those related to ethnic diversity are often described as 'controversial', 'might give rise to problems' or as 'a source of tension'. These are issues over which teachers are encouraged to take care and act with sensitivity.

The modern foreign languages working group suggested 'the appreciation and enjoyment of diversity' model as the way forward. The group also sees the broadening of learners' knowledge of the world and the promotion of the feeling for diversity as 'one of the prime aims of education'.

While all working groups 'feel' the need to reflect something of the contributions and achievements of minority ethnic groups to the curriculum, the ways in which this could be achieved pose a real problem. The mathematics group in our view contradicts itself. First it takes the decision not to include any multicultural aspects in any of the attainment targets. It then concedes that it would be important for teachers 'within the broad framework of the NC attainment targets and programmes of study, to select examples and materials which relate to the cultural background of their pupils'. In praise of an ethnically diverse school or classroom, the technology working group highlights the possible broadening of the insights and the range of appropriate and alternative solutions that a multi-ethnic class could bring to solving problems.

Not all the working groups were able to respond adequately to the question of the mono-ethnic classroom or school. In many ways this was reminiscent of the 'we have no ethnics here so we do not have the problem' syndrome. Teachers will have to ensure that those young people unfortunate enough not to be members of an ethnically diverse school gain some understanding of the cultural diversity of modern society.

A number of working groups seem to see the results of pursuing a gender equal opportunities policy in terms of access to good employment opportunities for girls, especially in fields where women are under-represented.

The definition of gender equal opportunities which finally prevails in the National Curriculum coincides with Nikki Fonda's 'open door' approach. At most, teachers are encouraged to help girls overcome their negative attitudes to subjects such as physical sciences and technology and to consider their course design and choice of materials to avoid bias. Girls are expected to become involved in traditionally male subjects, while traditionally female subjects remain optional in the National Curriculum, particularly at Key Stage 4. Only the Curriculum Guidance on Citizenship mentions sexism and sexual discrimination in the examples it provides, but these are not necessarily associated with the school.

However, the same is not said of multicultural education policies. They appear more as palliatives, which might at best improve tolerance of, and knowledge about, minorities.

It is clear from the working parties' reports that responses to an ethnically diverse society can be best pursued via multicultural education policies based on the notion of cultural pluralism/diversity.

However, two main aspects of this model appear to be in conflict with one another. On the one hand, there is the need to develop a greater understanding, respect and recognition for minority groups, while on the other is the need to preserve the 'natural' eurocentricity of the curriculum.

Hence the public debates over the content of the curriculum, and especially over history, mathematics, music and English. The publication of the NCC's art working group's interim report and advice to the Secretary of State was greeted with vitriolic outbursts from several public figures.

Professor Geoffrey Chew, lecturer and member of the Music Curriculum Association writing in *The Guardian* on 5 March 1991 claimed:

> ... buying these sitars, gamelans and so forth will cost the tax payer millions — for no discernible benefit, for in most schools there will be no one to discriminate between the important and the trivial, the good and the bad.

The then Secretary of State said:

> I cannot think of any other country where the dominant examples for study would not come from their own cultural tradition. I find it patronising and insulting that a child from a West Indian or Asian cultural background should not be able to come to gain pleasure from music from a West European background. They will be able to come to terms much better with the society in which they live if they do. (*The Guardian*, 25 January 1992)

The basis on which people were selected to be members of the working groups ensured much of the above.

The 5–16 documents preceded the Statutory Orders for the various National Curriculum subjects, and are no longer working documents, nor are they required reading for teachers. Yet these documents provide us with the most comprehensive coverage of equal opportunities issues.

The Non-Statutory Guidance and Curriculum Guidance series (the latter including the cross-curricular themes and dimensions) bear no force of law, but are by and large the remaining location of any mention of equal opportunities. The more detailed models for classroom implementation are set out in the guidance on the five cross-curricular themes.

*Curriculum Guidance 3* brings together the understanding of equal opportunities which appears in the 5–16 documents. In addition, equal opportunities is seen as a whole-school management issue in terms of policy, access and ethos, but again it is not clear how this guidance document stands in relation to the Statutory Orders for each subject.

Elsewhere in the Curriculum Guidance series, the five cross-curricular themes: Education for Economic and Industrial Understanding; Health Education: Careers Education: Environment Education: and Citizenship are outlined in detail. All make fleeting reference to equal opportunities, and despite ample scope to address equality issues, only the citizenship document provides any detailed references to cultural diversity.

Overall, the documents leave equal opportunities open to interpretation or omission. Furthermore, the general perception in schools is that the National Curriculum guidance is of much lesser significance than the subject Orders.

There is no consistency of equal opportunities across National Curriculum documents. For example, the Non-Statutory Guidance for science published in 1989 devoted several paragraphs to equal opportunities. It highlighted girls and pupils of ethnic minority origin as two groups who had not realized their full potential in the past. It was not sure that compulsory science in the National Curriculum would completely solve the problem, stating that 'the problems of low expectations of many girls, particularly in physical science, will remain' (para 7.5). Suggested action includes the appropriate design of courses and choice of materials.

In terms of race, the guidance highlighted the 'different interpretations of the view of science' which would be held by different ethnic groups. It addresses the possible language needs of minority ethnic learners and states that 'it is vital that ethnic or cultural bias is excluded from any activity' (para 7.7). The curriculum should reflect the contribution of different cultures to scientific enterprise, teaching materials should include examples of people from ethnic minority groups, and 'pupils should come to realize the international nature of science and the potential it has for helping to overcome racial prejudice' (para 7.8).

By contrast, there is no mention of equal opportunities either in the Statutory Orders or in the Non-Statutory Guidance for maths. The absence of race equality is consistent with the argument set out in *Mathematics for Ages 5–16*, that a 'multicultural' approach to mathematics, with children being introduced to different numeral systems, foreign currencies and non-European measuring and counting devices, could confuse young children. The silence on both race and gender in the final Orders, as well as the above comments, is in direct conflict with the final Orders for science. However, the low expectations of girls are equally well documented in both subjects, and the origins of the subject in different cultures and its possible contribution to overcoming racial prejudice, as well as other issues outlined in the science Orders, apply equally to that of maths.

Educationalists working in the field of equal opportunities raise questions relating to the 'hidden' as well as the 'overt' curriculum in discussing how schools may attempt to address equality issues. It could be argued that pedagogy, apparently still left to the individual school and teacher, is the area where further work for equality can and should take place. It is worth heeding Bruce Gill's suggestion:

> Pedagogy can be said to be critical to the process — leading one to speculate whether an important intended purpose for assessment is to function less as a measure of pupil performance and more as a mechanism to temper teacher intervention. (Gill, 1991, pp. 134–46)

Although it is not intended to look at assessment in detail here, it is worth noting some of the equal opportunities issues which relate to assessment, and which will impinge on the teaching of the National Curriculum in schools.

One of the major uses of the tests is to produce league tables of schools, which, it is claimed, will help parents to select the right school for their children. Chitty, Jakubowska and Jones, in their analysis on the changing direction of National Curriculum Assessment explain:

> This means that tests, and the curriculum which is the basis of the tests, have to be planned with a view to providing information which can be easily summarized and publicized in the form of scores, and of league tables based on these scores. (Chitty, Jakubowska and Jones, 1991, pp. 83–99)

The difficulties teachers faced in introducing the Standard Assessment Tasks in 1991 provided John Major with an ideal opportunity to announce that they would be replaced in 1992 with paper and pencil Standard Assessment Tests. In addition to the effect that 'teaching to the test' will have on classroom pedagogy, there are major concerns to be addressed relating to culture and gender bias in written tests, and the way girls' and boys' performance is affected differently by this form of assessment.

It seems likely that schools will resort to setting and streaming, if they are not already doing this, in order to maximize their chances in the league table. Presumably this will in future be done on the basis of previous SAT results, and will therefore perpetuate the biased outcomes of the crude form of testing which has been applied. Disapplication from the National Curriculum, and therefore from the test, also seems likely, in order to boost schools' rankings.

Already there is an increase in demand for the statementing of children with special educational needs and in the number of pupil exclusions. Again Bruce Gill reminds us that black pupils have a history of educational experience in language centres, special needs schools and on suspension. We can only speculate on how many black pupils will be disapplied, as it is not a figure which schools are required to publish.

Finally, we should point out that different parts of the National Curriculum will be assessed differently. There will not be Standard Assessment Tasks or Tests for all subjects; music, art and PE will be assessed using only end of key stage statements written by the teacher. There is no statutory method of assessment for religious education or the cross-curricular themes. We can go no further than raise the issues as cause for concern, not least about consistency across the curriculum.

## Managing Equal Opportunities

A major issue a school must face is how it is going to 'manage' equal opportunities in the National Curriculum, and in the whole curriculum. Below is a list of some of the things a school and teachers would be expected to do in order to effectively teach the National Curriculum and secure equal opportunities (the list is drawn from the Non-Statutory Guidance and Orders):

(i) to develop clear criteria for the selection of materials;

(ii) to select materials which reflect the diversity of cultures represented in the school (and in society at large);

(iii) to help children to use those materials to demonstrate what they can do;

(iv) not to present European and Western materials as superior to other forms;

(v) to recognize, explore and use materials, tasks and activities which reflect pupils' first hand experience of life and their own histories;

(vi) to design and use activities and programmes which enable all pupils to develop qualities and skills relating to cooperation, sensitivity, fair play and tolerance;

(vii) to plan activities which are acceptable to pupils of all religious affiliations — respecting cultural norms and religious observances;

(viii) to select and use visitors from a diverse range of cultural and ethnic backgrounds as well as women in non-traditional jobs;

(ix) to have knowledge of the needs and concerns of various ethnic groups;

(x) to help pupils to recognize and challenge stereotyping and to detect bias: and

(xi) to use language which does not stop pupils from gaining access to the curriculum.

The emphasis throughout the documentation is on teachers selecting and using materials, tasks and people in order to further the cause of equal opportunities. They must also be able, through their teaching, to help children to challenge certain aspects of racism and sexism. We remain unconvinced that there are enough teachers (and schools), with the knowledge base, who can critically assess, select materials and teach about the issues.

The evidence to date is that equal opportunities issues are not central to schools and teaching. Generally, schools have not reacted positively to equal opportunities. A number of researchers and writers (Troyna and Williams, 1986; Troyna and Carrington, 1990) have all pointed to the 'superficial, cosmetic and at times opportunistic nature of some multicultural policies'. Other criticisms have located the problems in the institutions and the individuals within them, some of whom have been incapable, unwilling or doggedly resistant to developing anti-racist/sexist approaches to the curriculum.

Many teachers and schools perceive the implementation of the National Curriculum as a burden on their time, energy and resources. There is evidence that equal opportunities issues are regarded as difficult to deal with on a personal level. How can teachers help children to challenge sexist/racist language, or stereotyping without first understanding and accepting how they as individuals have values and ways of behaving which have been informed by racism and sexism? Do teachers understand what racism and sexism are and how they manifest themselves in the curriculum and in the school?

Schools are often places of contradictions where race and gender issues are concerned. On the one hand, the stated aims might be about promoting equal opportunities, while on the other the underlying values, ethos and practice belie equality. The treatment of the issues in the National Curriculum gives schools a framework for confused and contradictory thinking and practice. It does not provide schools with the tools with which to analyze fundamental issues around 'the relationships between class, culture and educational achievement'. Neither does it demand from schools the kinds of understanding and clear commitment teachers would need in order to tackle 'successfully the core issue of inequality'. Indeed, the development of policies on the basis of the frameworks presented throughout the National Curriculum documentation is likely to stagnate developments in equality.

Those of us who have long been involved in anti-racist, anti-sexist education feel that the proposals and subsequent references contained in some of the Statutory Orders and Non-Statutory Guidance do not address race, class and gender inequalities. The core issues remain untouched. A 'cultural diversity' and 'access to opportunities' approach does not allow for a critical analysis of the existing power relationships. Although appearing to be promoting equal opportunities, some would argue that this approach is nothing but a wolf in sheep's clothing.

Many educationalists have followed a policy of 'constructive engagement'. This strategy has succeeded in defending even in developing some good practice, but it has been followed at the expense of a larger vision of educational purpose. (Chitty *et al.*, p. 89)

If we do have such a vision, then to argue for schools to develop equal opportunities policies on the basis of the frameworks presented in the documentation would be a foolish proposal.

There is perhaps still remaining a vision of education based on equality and justice. The development of such a vision is best achieved by involving all the partners in the school: teachers, pupils, parents, governors and the wider community — all of whom have been disenfranchized from the process of developing the present National Curriculum.

## References

CHITTY, C., JAKUBOWSKA, T. and JONES, K. (1991) 'The National Curriculum and Assessment: Changing course' *in* Millcole group, *Changing the Future*, London, Tufnell Press, pp. 85–99.

DES (1989) National Curriculum: *From Policy to Practice*, London, DES.

FONDA, N. (1989) 'Equal opportunities in TVEI: The Fonda typology', *Gender Equality, From Analysis to Action*, pp. 47–9.

GILL, B. (1991) 'Pedagogy and assessment', *Multicultural Teaching*, 10, 1.

TROYNA, B. and WILLIAMS, J. (1986) *Racism, education and the state*, London, Croom Helm.

TROYNA, B. and CARRINGTON, B. (1990) *Education, racism and reform*, London, Routledge.

*Chapter 6*

# The National Curriculum in a Secondary School

*Alan Leech*

No-one can examine the National Curriculum's operation and implementation at secondary school level without an awareness of the climate under which schools have been working since 1988. The Education Reform Act was a great and powerful force for change and both the tidal wave and ripple effect of the changes triggered have yet to cease. In particular, schools have been adjusting to and amending their operations with regard to Local Management of Schools (LMS) at same time as dealing with the staged introduction of the National Curriculum and national testing. These twin, and eventually linked, developments have posed severe problems for schools in reviewing, modifying and formulating policies. LMS has the dual thrusts of formula funding and much devolved management. At the same time, schools have had to deal with the most radical and far-reaching changes in curriculum organization, planning and delivery that present-day staff have ever known. In addition, schools have had newly constituted governing bodies, with wider but different responsibilities, a more diverse membership, an increase in powers, and an increase in size. Further, schools have had to deal with a new Pay and Conditions Document which has arrived annually, each time with amendments to aspects of a school's operation, such as discretionary pay, which have often been largely unclear and confusing to headteachers and governors. More recently, to add to the pressure of changes, teacher and headteacher appraisal has been introduced.

Change has been substantial. Each school has been affected in a different way. LMS has been staged, with no two LEAs adopting the same practices or time scale; the National Curriculum is being staged over several years. For some schools, however, all the changes have taken place simultaneously and posed considerable operational and planning problems. The fact that these have been quietly and expeditiously dealt with says much for the quality and resilience of school management and the teacher teams who have worked with commitment and diligence to maintain all existing programmes whilst adjusting to the changes flowing from the Act. Much good, positive and impressive work and associated policies have characterized developments in schools as they have come to terms with change and the need to do so in a professional manner which affords the best opportunities for young people.

## The Curriculum

The National Curriculum at school level has to be seen at both the macro and micro level; both demand careful and detailed management if implementation is to be as straightforward as possible. The macro level relates to the whole school perspective with its view of the staged introduction of each subject, the position of cross-curricular schemes, and the relationship to the school culture or ethos. It also includes time considerations: the whole school week, the distribution of lessons by individual subject, and the allocation of resources in the form of teaching, non-teaching personnel, plus money for books, equipment and in-service training. On the other hand, the micro level relates to the work of the individual National Curriculum subject, which in secondary schools is operated through an individual subject department. Issues at this level include: the number of teachers needed to teach successfully and implement fully the subject; the amount of money devolved to the department for books, equipment and so on; the number, type and quality of rooms available for subject delivery; the amount of non-contact time available to teachers each week; the amount of planning and preparation time made available prior to the introduction of the subject. It is abundantly clear that no consideration of the National Curriculum can take place in isolation from the other major policy changes in schools. For instance, LMS with its major planning possibilities for spending prioritization involves a focussed approach to linking aims to the delivery of the National Curriculum and offers the scope to identify, plan and then implement the programmes of action necessary.

## School Developments: Macro Level

The National Curriculum has provided a spur for all schools to look at what they are offering not only in curriculum terms, but also in regard to the experience each pupil receives. This has unquestionably been beneficial, though hard and time-consuming. It has been made more difficult by the volume of other changes schools have handled and has strained the abilities of staff already dealing with a myriad of systems adjustments.

The introduction of the concept of a development plan, as a planning tool, has been welcome — though recognized as a difficult and complex operation to undertake in a bold or realistic three-five year sort of way. Suggestions sometimes made about the lack of long-term planning are an insult to all who manage at school level. Planning is relatively easy, or at least logically straightforward if budget stability can be assured, if additional governmental

Figure 6.1: Operation of the National Curriculum in schools

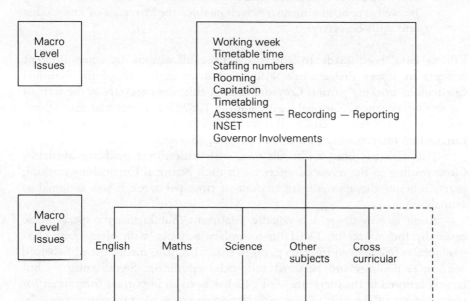

initiatives can be anticipated, and if information on the staging of the National Curriculum and its associated tests at 7, 11, 14 and 16 was reliable, consistent, or in some cases, simply available.

Nevertheless, the idea that we should, at Key Stage 3, audit our curriculum and especially the experience of pupils, is an important and significant development for the school system. Questions to be asked include:

● Is the balance of time between subjects right?
● Are we covering each subject in sufficient depth to enable it to provide a stimulating, worthwhile and meaningful experience for each pupil, regardless of ability?

• Do we have the necessary range of expertise to enable each subject to be well taught in a manner which enables the coverage of knowledge and skills necessary?

Efforts have been made to adjust the time allocations between different subjects in a way that accords with the known intentions of the National Curriculum working parties. Consideration of this was necessary at the start of the secondary school National Curriculum in 1989 (for science and maths), but has become a must to enable the introduction of the last of the National Curriculum subjects of art, music and physical education in 1992.

This task has been a difficult one, with little direct guidance available. Close reading of the terms of reference of each National Curriculum working party indicates the approximate amount of time per week it was assumed as available.

Audit at Key Stage 4 is equally important, but in many respects made easier by the impact of TVEI on secondary schools, with often quite clear guidance as to the need for each pupil to study English, maths, broad/balanced science, technology and personal and social education. Significantly — but largely ignored in the literature — TVEI has been an important forerunner for some aspects of the principle of prescription in terms of curriculum operation and delivery.

In planning for Key Stage 4 it has been important, too, to examine the current and possible allocation of timetable time to youngsters in years 10 and 11. How can the National Curriculum subjects fit into the existing time? Will it be compulsory for every National Curriculum subject to be studied, and if so, how would they fit into a teaching week? Unfortunately, for good planning, the answers to some of these questions have taken some time to move towards an operational pattern that embraces all that they statutorily need to provide. This pattern will need to include compulsory and non-compulsory subjects and whole and part GCSE courses. Time is on the side of the schools in this, for a full operational pattern will not be needed for year 10 until September 1995.

Associated with the range of subjects in secondary schools, and the proportion of the school teaching week devoted to each, is the question of the, as yet, variable nature of the length of the school day. Up to now the DES has not enacted regulations to deal with this, but has instead recommended — through *Circular 7/90* — minimum teaching times (excluding tutorials, registration and assemblies) as follows:

|  | **Hours per week** | **Hours per day** |
|---|---|---|
| KS3 and KS4 | 24 | 4.8 |

Schools would be advised to only revise their lesson times and hence the totality of the school day in the light of the fullest knowledge of the requirements at Key Stage 4, since to adjust one without regard to the other would be a serious mistake.

### School Developments: Micro Level

No one subject experience typifies the introduction of the National Curriculum at the micro level. This is because each subject is different in content, range of attainment targets, and because of the piecemeal or staged introduction of subjects. For instance, in secondary schools the phasing of the National Curriculum subjects has been in stages since 1989 on the basis of two, two, two and four subjects introduced to successive year 7 children.

The management of the school needs to be highly sensitive to, and aware of, each departmental area so that the introduction can be as smooth and efficient as possible. School-wide curriculum coordinators such as the Headteacher, or a Deputy, need to have read the National Curriculum documents relating to any subject which is about to be implemented. They need to understand the language, the proportion of the timetabled time indicated as a sensible allocation, the extent to which it helps fit into any cross-curricular work, and the type of methods of assessment associated with the subject. The same sort of reading and understanding inevitably must characterize the work at departmental level. Some questions to ask include:

- How does the curriculum match that at present in operation in the school?
- How should the curriculum be staged over the three Key Stage 3 years?
- What teaching materials will be needed to deliver the subject?
- Are any new materials needed to replace or amend areas of study previously dealt with in the school?
- What will be the net cost of introducing the curriculum?
- Are there specialist teacher skills required for staff, over and above those available at present?
- Does each department have any INSET targets that can be identified as arising from the National Curriculum?
- How should a teaching programme be constructed, and with what materials for the teaching groups within a department?
- What information is known about the kind of tests to be applied by law at the end of the key stage?
- How should routine and regular assessment of children's work be undertaken?
- What sort of pupil and parent reporting process could and should be applied to the subject, and how might this fit in with the overall policy of the school?

The posing of questions such as these is relatively easy — but how much systematic work of this type is actually undertaken must be regarded as unclear. Research on planning of this type is complicated and time-consuming. In many respects this is an area for LEA inspectors and advisers to lead on and offer assistance. However, such is the lack of precision as to the kind of operational role they should undertake at LEA level, with the division between inspecting and advising, that a clear opportunity to work collaboratively area-wide is all too often being lost. Each school must, seek its own salvation to the National Curriculum introduction. To accomplish this satisfactorily will necessitate a good team spirit, high morale, quality leadership from each head of department, positive cooperation and time.

The use of time is a major operational issue. Problems of its sufficiency pose a serious obstacle to the fullest development of the National Curriculum. The Pay and Conditions Document defines 'directed' time and five professional days as available for the fullest utilization. Yet, such has been the growth of initiatives launched by central government since 1988 which impact upon schools that the available amounts of time have been seriously eroded. It is thus a major planning issue for schools to face: how to make available enough time to enable groups of teachers to come together to read, present papers, write, compare analyses, phase syllabus implementation, agree grade standards for pupils' work, cross-moderate — teacher by teacher — and explain to colleagues, pupils and parents about the purpose and extent of the developments they are overseeing. If it is difficult at the subject department level, it is a much more severe problem at the level of cross-curricular developments, since here analysis needs to be across several subjects and involve teachers belonging to disparate subject teams across the school.

There is no panacea for the time problem. It must be faced head on and teachers need to be encouraged to manage that which is available in the most advantageous way possible. The head, and others with school-wide responsibilities need to be aware of the issues, show empathy by their readings, attendance at departmental meetings and personal contacts. Imaginative approaches can be sought to the problem. These can be applied to departments facing pre-implementation work and also actual operational work devoted to the new subject in hand. These approaches can include:

(i) Release teachers in groups, or the whole departmental team on an agreed number of occasions from teaching in order to allow them to work on planning matters. The finance for this could come by virement from within the existing school budget, and supply teachers hired. This possibility is easily available under LMS, provided the school's budget share was sufficient initially.

(ii) Utilize intensively as possible the time released within school following the departure of year 11 or 13 students in June and July. This time has always been very valuable: it is now crucial to school management.

(iii) Use time to assemble teacher working parties on occasions when large groups of pupils are not on the school site for a particular reason. For example, under the terms of TVEI all secondary pupils undertake work experience for one or two weeks.

(iv)   Plan to use the five professional days in the most effective way possible for National Curriculum planning work.

The only way imaginative uses of time can be contemplated fully is if there is sufficient and clear rapport at both the micro and macro levels of the school. A commitment, aligned to a clear vision of the demands facing teachers and departmental heads is paramount.

## The Overall School Plan

Though the challenges of the National Curriculum are considerable, its introduction, year on year, has offered considerable scope for a reappraisal of existing policies and practices at school and departmental level. Arising from considerations at departmental level will come an examination of teaching methodology, the importance of working as a team, a reduction of individual anonymity and/or autonomy, and a revision of what sort of curriculum diet is currently on offer in each and every school.

These changes arise because in every school staff know they need to make sure their teaching programme accords with the National Curriculum, covers the attainment targets and is capable of being assessed at the end of the key stage. It seems likely, given the kind of teamwork necessary to undertake the task in hand, that more rigorous teaching programmes may well follow, together with a reformulation of materials in use. Review, revision and reform are all key to the successful operation of a National Curriculum subject. Desirable and beneficial outcomes to date include the following:

- modifications to the efficiency of whole-school planning;
- improvements in the management of curriculum delivery and hence the curriculum experience of the pupil;
- greater information on the true costs of operating the curriculum;
- a closer linkage between the school priorities and the curriculum needs of pupils; and
- an improvement in the collaborative work of teachers at departmental and whole school level; with a strengthening of the concept of partnership and an emphasis on cooperation.

Another inevitable consequence relates to the governing body. Given the legal responsibilities of the governors, and bearing in mind the complexity and rapidity of change, it will be essential for members to be aware of developments in train. Information should relate not only to a description but also deal with staffing, INSET and the overall financial demands upon the school.

### Cross-curricular Issues

Cross-curricular work — that is work that it is intended to be provided as part of the school's operation for all children, but is not part of any named subject or timetabled slot — is very important and must not be lost from sight.

Before the National Curriculum was laid down by statute and defined subjects were introduced, all schools would claim that not only did they provide those specific subjects but also that they offered a wealth of cross-curricular activities as part of the experience of each child. Despite the claims, provision was, and remains, variable. Yet, there is an assumption that in a high quality education cross-curricular elements will exist.

To help schools in their planning and to support schools where extensive cross-curricular work already existed the National Curriculum Council and the Curriculum Council for Wales have published booklets designed to show a range of cross-curriculum dimensions, skills and themes which they believe should be included in the curriculum experience of all pupils. The work includes equal opportunities for all pupils, irrespective of ethnic background, culture, gender or ability, and accommodating outline techniques for dealing with communication, study skills, problem-solving, personal and social skills, and information technology. Work on these areas should permeate the whole school, and can in some instances be delivered by tutorial activities or as part of the overall ethos.

Dealing with cross-curricular themes is a major organizational problem, which has been little addressed in any practical sense. Managerially, when the bulk of timetabled time has been allocated to specific and clearly defined National Curriculum subjects, to find a vehicle for the planning, implementation and operation of additional national curriculum themes or dimensions is difficult. The booklets from the NCC and CCW are readable, interesting and useful. Nevertheless, how to deliver remains an issue of significance. Some of the management challenges can be outlined as follows:

(i) The identification of a person centrally in school who will read and assess a booklet on a cross-curricular theme and examine which components within which National Curriculum subjects can be said to be delivering the theme outlined. Since the topic is one which in a secondary school will extend over a full five years, it is also necessary to examine which bits should go where.

(ii) Find time to allow a group of teachers responsible for the teaching of a specific range of National Curriculum subjects to come together to discuss not only where they are to deliver the statutory subject but also cross-curricular dimensions as well.

(iii) Find a mechanism for 'tracking' cross-curricular work. This approach would need data to be collected at some central point, away from each department responsible for subject delivery.

(iv) There would be a need for information to flow two-way from department(s) to centre and centre to department(s) if progress were to be monitored and an analysis of policy implementation to be undertaken.

(v) Teachers involved in such a cross-curricular development would need to meet, from time to time, to review progress, redefine the programme and assess the attainment of children.

Unresolved issues arising from cross-curricular work include: reporting to parents, coordination and time for inter-subject meetings. Equally, since cross-curricular subjects are not enshrined in regulation, and do not feature as part of the published performance information required under the 1992 Education Act, their position as consumers of time and energy might well be in jeopardy. A prioritization of time to see to it that high quality efficient systems for the operation of cross-curricular work are in place seems unlikely. Much valuable work that has permeated many schools' pastoral guidance systems, and has featured as part of TVEI developments on personal and social education may well be damaged.

The management problem of cross-curricular work is considerable. Time will tell whether getting to grips with such work is prioritized within a school.

## Assessment Recording and Reporting

The content, style and delivery of the National Curriculum is only one aspect of its operation in schools. In addition, there is a requirement to put into place a simple, unambiguous and clear policy on the assessment of children's progress and the recording of that progress as well as a methodology for reporting both to parents and to children the standards reached. Insufficient attention has been given to this element of the National Curriculum and yet it is highly important if the fullest benefits in raising standards are to be gained.

The National Curriculum, with its precision and highly directed centralist approach needs to be accompanied by modifications in the assessment policies of each school. Firstly, this is necessary because of the laid down, but as yet tentatively defined, attainment levels 1–10 and the need to report on children's attainment using these numerical figures at 7, 11, 14 and 16. Secondly, it is important to make adjustments to existing policies because of the vagaries, subjectivity and lack of known definition associated with many school or subject departmental practices. Examples include: What does C+ mean? 31st out of 33 pupils in a year group in English at an independent girls' school was one report seen recently for a 13-year-old. Very good, average, unsatisfactory: they are all historically well-used words to describe pupil performance, but all lack any rigour or objectivity.

The major problems in producing a school or departmental policy on assessment for a secondary school include some of the following:

(i) The statutory grading requirements at 14 and 16 of levels 1—10 condition what can be done at any other age than these.

(ii) Explaining in any meaningful sort of way the range of possible levels of performance that will be achieved by each pupil at the end of each key stage and the relationship of these to earlier key stages, bearing in mind that the same grading levels apply to all four stages — even when applied to different types of work in a particular subject.

(iii) Whether to use levels 1—10 for any year group other than years 9 and 11 in their end of year report, and whether to apply these levels to individual pieces of work.

(iv) How to define what a particular level actually is or appears to look like. For instance, what is the standard of work of a pupil in, say, geography in year 9 which will result in the award of a level 6 and what different piece of work will justify the same level 6 in the GCSE at the end of year 11 based upon different work and different skills?

(v) Inter-teacher moderation of marking standards. Should moderation at departmental level be on the basis of every piece of work marked, only occasionally sampled work, or only end of key stage work?

(vi) If levels of attainment on the 1—10 scale were applied widely other than at the end of years 9 and 11, then, given the low levels of performance achieved by the majority of the child population (in numerical terms), there is a possibility of a demotivating and demoralizing effect upon pupils.

(vii) If the 1—10 levels were not used routinely, then a standardized objective marking scheme would need to be utilized within a department in order to record accurately the progress made and the attainment achieved as well as signifying future actions necessary. This approach would demand written comments from teachers and make no use of levels or grades as measures of attainment.

Such considerations as above are desirable and necessary ingredients in the work of all schools. If children are not to receive misleading, inaccurate or incomplete information (as they did before the National Curriculum with its 1—10 levels) a careful matching of teacher assessment and written comments will be necessary, together with the most careful use of attainment level figures at years 7 and 11.

The recording of pupils' performance will also pose significant management and operational issues for all schools. If the routine reporting of attainments to pupils is largely on the basis of written comments, how can teachers translate that into National Curriculum attainment levels in their mark books or computer record systems? One way has been to add to the teacher's note about a particular piece of work a level range, i.e. 3—5 or 4—7 in relation

performance rather than a prec... need to be done to devise the b... ...ording progress.

With regard to the reporting element... clearer since the DES has produced a pos... *Circular 5/92* makes clear the obligations of... requirement for schools is to produce an annu... Curriculum attainment levels at the end of years... Separate school-by-school decisions are still requ... more than one report each year, whether to give... than the overall level for the subject, on the basis... Each school has, therefore, a high level of flexibility o... to decide how to react on the basis of its commitmen... mation to parents and pupils, its view of accountabil... balance demands on staff against possible wasteful work w... ate rather than stimulate pupils' attitudes and performance...

The field of assessment, recording and reporting is... continue to need attention in the years ahead as schools seek... requirements, accountability, time, pupil motivation and infor... against management issues such as moderation, record syste... production.

## Conclusion

The changes following the 1988 Education Reform Act have b... and far-reaching. The work expected of, and accomplished by,... management teams in school has been vast. Research, analysis, ex... implementation possibilities, prioritization, selection of action... then implementation has been the order of the day in all loca... schools. Much good practice has occurred as whole tracts of the... have been re-examined and re-planned. Drive, inventiveness and... clear leadership have been important characteristics of school life...

Unresolved operational issues still remain, such as the plac... modern foreign language, the value accorded cross-curricular v... opment of assessment policies, how to record, and, equally in... to report. Still to face is the full operation of Key Stage 3... Finally, resolution is awaited of the whole pattern of Key S... and vocational courses, and the kind of teaching times neces... subjects.

Schools are inventive, innovative places. If they were... handling of all that has been introduced since 1988 could n...

*Part 3*

# *Perspectives from LEAs*

*Chapter 7*

---

# The LEA and the National Curriculum

---

*Jennifer Wisker*

The Education Reform Act has meant a significant change in the role and responsibilities of the local education authority (LEA). Inevitably one must ask the question: does the advent of self-managed schools, whether they stay within the orbit of the LEA or seek grant maintained status, together with a nationally determined curriculum, mean that the LEA's future role will be negligible? Will the LEA, like unpopular schools, be left to wither on the vine? If not, what direction should the LEA take and what should be its future role?

In practice, a forward-looking LEA has been anticipating the changes encapsulated in the 1988 Education Reform Act over the last decade. Many have been actively encouraging self-managed schools prior to the introduction of local management, by delegating substantial budgets to them. Schools as cost centres were operating by the early 1980s in several county authorities. Therefore, supporting schools and their governing bodies in carrying out their responsibilities has been a key LEA role, involving several professional disciplines: education, finance, property, personnel and legal services. That role of support has, of course, been accelerated by the 1988 Act and subsequent changes which have allowed all schools to become locally managed.

Similarly, with regard to the National Curriculum, LEAs have been preparing for its advent and, consequently, their changing role, again over a period of time. As early as 1977, LEAs were requested to report on their curricular arrangements. The provision within the 1986 Act that they have a curriculum policy culminated with the introduction of the National Curriculum itself in 1988. An important element underpinning those developments was central Government support for in-service education and training of teachers via specific grants, together with specific curricular initiatives supported by education support grants, now brought together under the GEST (Grants for Education Support and Training) programme. In reality, as far as LEAs were concerned, this meant that the Government nationally was determining its priorities by earmarking specifically 2 per cent of local government expenditure. If LEAs did not bid for these special projects authorities lost that 2 per cent in any event from their overall funding. Successful authorities, however, often succeeded in getting more than their share. The advantage of specific grant, as far as the Chief Education Officer is concerned, is that the funds are earmarked and cannot be used elsewhere to support a council's expenditure; the disadvantage is that this has meant to a greater extent that the role of the LEA is implementer, not simply of local priorities, but for those that are determined nationally. Yet the GEST programmes and the programmes which preceded it gave LEAs, in my view, an unrivalled opportunity to concentrate on curriculum development to a degree which had not been possible before. Developments in maths, science and English predated and, to a large extent, underpinned, the implementation of the National Curriculum. That the latter has gone relatively smoothly is, to a large extent, dependent on earlier groundwork and support of LEA INSET programmes.

A similar development which has predated and run alongside the implementation of the National Curriculum has been the establishment of various schemes funded by the Department of Employment under various nomenclatures. What has been crucial, however, has been the impact of the Technical and Vocational Education Initiative (TVEI). It brought the role of technology to the forefront and in particular its role in underpinning the curriculum as a whole. Indeed, although National Curriculum design and technology is seen as a new curriculum area, TVEI has undoubtedly assisted the implementation of the philosophy as well as the practice. Without the LEA as initiator, implementer, as well as key partner, the passage could well have been less smooth.

So, since well before the implementation of the National Curriculum, LEAs have been used to working within new partnerships. There was active cooperation by several authorities with HMI in the 1980s, which identified key curricular areas of experience which were to be the entitlement of all pupils: areas which when translated into subjects bear a close resemblance to the core and foundation subjects of the National Curriculum today. Similarly, on the primary side, HMI in their survey in 1978 identified several of the key issues which needed to be addressed nationally and locally — differentiation, leadership in terms of the curriculum and overall management plus the use of non-contact time — are all areas which have been highlighted in the recent discussion document on primary education. An uncomfortable question for LEAs, training authorities and national Government must be why are these still identified as issues by the Alexander, Rose and Woodhead report fifteen years later? Has it taken a formalized curriculum by statute to make us act at national, LEA and school level?

What the introduction of the National Curriculum has done is to change the role of local authority advisory and inspection services and, of course, HMI. That this was evident even before the recent proposals in the 1992 Schools Act can be seen as a direct consequence of the shift in power and responsibility in terms of governance from LEA to school governors which is why, in my view, the clauses of the Education Reform Act relating to the curriculum, local management and grant maintained status are virtually inextricable.

As was highlighted by the Audit Commission in their national survey in 1989 on the role of inspectors and advisers and reinforced by a number of local audits, my own Authority included, was the need to ensure more systematic management and greater accountability for the inspection service as a whole. This meant clear role identification, systematic inspection and advice to schools: a knowledge of how schools functioned and all aspects of management as opposed to advice on curriculum developments and support of specialist curriculum areas on a fairly random basis. For many authorities with a clear view of inspection the recommended changes were not new. For many, however, it meant a fairly dramatic change of role, function and responsibility.

The dual role of inspection linked with advice has helped schools with the introduction of the National Curriculum at Key Stages 1 and 2. I would question whether without it schools would have embraced the National Curriculum as positively as they have done, or would be prepared to discuss and highlight its difficulties in the shorter and longer term.

LEAs, through their advisory and inspection services have given advice and support to schools as the core and foundation subjects have come on stream. Working parties were set up to ensure LEA guidance to schools on the introduction of the National Curriculum was helpful and relevant. Joint courses were run between the Authority and providing institutions to improve teachers' own subject knowledge, for example in science. In addition, practical support has been given by several LEAs in terms of resources over and above what has been allocated nationally. My own Authority has regularly contributed £1 million a year to support the curriculum, which is considerable when looked at in the context of an Authority tight up against its capping levels. This has been spent on additional supply support, largely for primary schools, and was particularly useful during the Key Stage 1 assessments. Secondary schools had benefited earlier from additional resources made available with the introduction of GCSE, which remains in the base budget.

Looking ahead, I see a role for the LEA as the National Curriculum comes on stream, not just in terms of support for the core and foundation subjects, but also in supporting and implementing changes and modifications to programmes of study and attainment targets, and in the implementation of that part of the Education Reform Act which relates to the moral, aesthetic and spiritual dimension of the curriculum and preparation for adult life.

Nevertheless, the balance of power has moved from the LEA to the school governors. This has been recognized in Somerset through our approach to curriculum review, inspection and teacher appraisal where we endeavour to work in partnership with schools in monitoring and evaluating the quality of the education provided. Obviously quantitative data, exam results, average costs, are important in establishing the performance of the school, but it is supported by evaluation based on classroom and task observation which is even more significant in determining the value which is added to each student's learning experience.

The purposes of inspection are common. There is an obligation to the taxpayer as well as the direct consumer to monitor the education provided. All inspections, whether those currently provided by the LEA and those to be provided in the future once approved by HMCI must look at the curriculum as experienced by the individual student, the overall education and provision of each establishment, the management of the establishment within a local authority or a grant maintained context.

The inspection will need to consider those measures of pupil achievement which are readily available, but above all should consider the quality of pupils' learning. All other factors must be seen in relation to that; leadership at all levels; the efficiency and effectiveness of management and organization; the management and delivery of the curriculum; the quality of staff development and the outcomes of internal or external teacher appraisal; the overall environment and ethos; teaching methods and approaches; differentiation; the extent of parental involvement in learning and governance of the school; the effectiveness of the school's internal review procedures; an assessment of the school's own internal performance indicators. Any evaluation must start with the curriculum, but will involve others in the evaluation of the effectiveness of delegation through local management. A school will need to show a clear linkage between its policy, as expressed through the School Development Plan, its needs, its resources and its results in terms of standards pupils achieve.

Of course, outside the formal inspection schools may well wish to buy in support for specific issues facing them, for example, management issues, budget presentation to governors, the overall use of resources, the link between teacher appraisal and the overall performance of the school as well as such technical issues as marketing, communication, finance, personnel and property management.

Inspection, advice, curriculum development and support will be functions which an LEA team comprised of advisers, inspectors and officers from other disciplines will be well placed to offer. The financial viability of such a team will need to be closely examined, given that much of the funding will be devolved to schools for inspection and other purposes. Whether a team is best placed as an integral part of an LEA or as a separate company undertaking work for a variety of clients, one of whom could be the LEA, needs to be worked out. Such a team, however, could undertake the quadrennial inspections to enable governing bodies to meet the requirements of HMCI; it could give schools advice on school development plans; on follow-up from quadrennial inspections and on staff development. In addition, the LEA will need such a team to monitor the curriculum; ensure that public funds are being used effectively by governing bodies and deal with any complaints of noncompliance with the National Curriculum.

Once schools overcome the technicalities of local management they will see that in order to maintain and, more significantly, demonstrate quality to their users and customers, namely their parents and students, they will need to manage the school through the curriculum and ensure improvements in the quality of teaching and learning in the classroom. LEAs, through their own inspection teams or teams brought in, could offer that support to their own schools. A similar service could be offered to grant maintained schools and, indeed, to independent schools.

Schools are becoming increasingly conscious that devolution of funding brings important responsibilities. The legal requirement to deliver the National Curriculum and to publicize assessment results means that they are being faced not just with the responsibility for quality, but also the need to demonstrate clearly that it is being achieved. At the same time, competition can lead them to isolation from the LEA and its advice and support, isolation from the comfort and stimulus of contacts with other schools; isolation from the sources of professional development which enable those managing schools to help colleagues meet the various legal requirements. In addition, many schools, particularly smaller ones, are losing the benefit of the economies of scale, and it is difficult to see in a large rural county authority, how small primary schools will be able to find the resources of time, money and expertise to formulate and carry out effectively the necessary staff development which is crucial if teaching and learning programmes are to improve. The likely increase in the number of schools seeking grant maintained status, while increasing opportunities for some of those schools, will certainly exacerbate problems.

It is understandable that many heads express concern. There is a marked increase in their responsibility for identifying development needs, and planning and securing the fulfilment of those needs is accompanied in many cases by a marked decrease in the ability to purchase expert advice and training. For example, to whom can a head turn when there is concern about the quality of teaching and learning, for example, in a specific area of the curriculum like English, or when there is anxiety about the inadequacy of health and safety procedures or financial systems? Will it be from the LEA or an LEA-linked consultancy that a head can best obtain sound, dispassionate, professional advice and effective support?

It was an effort to meet these various new requirements which prompted Somerset as an authority, as a result of lengthy consultations with heads, to put together all the professional development and support services in one unit, called the Professional Development Unit. This unit endeavours to meet the training and development needs of all the LEA's staff, teachers, lecturers, support staff, senior managers in schools and colleges, governors and Education Department staff. It is much more cost-effective than what existed previously, and it means that professional development can be delivered in an increasingly cohesive, flexible way. The use of information collated from schools' development plans, from county-wide appraisal targets and from school inspections enables the Professional Development Unit to offer the support and development opportunities which schools require. The agenda, therefore, has shifted from being that of the LEA to that of the school.

Looking ahead, it would seem that when the recruitment, retention and motivation of teachers is obviously at the top of any agenda, it should be possible for an authority to devise with key school representatives an incremental career-long professional development programme with certificated stages covering of self-management, classroom management, curriculum management and personnel management. Schools would have the opportunity to buy into the programme and the certificate so that their teachers would be able to key into the appropriate stage when they and the school deemed fit. Such a scheme may be complicated to work out and, of course, to accredit, but it would constitute an attractive inducement to teachers to come into the area and would endorse the LEA's commitment to staff training and development. Prototypes of this type of pattern already exist in some parts of the country.

The creation of the PDU is an example of Somerset's approach of extended delegation of resources to schools which has, of course, considerable implication for the organization of the authority as a whole and not simply the Education Department. Schools are given the option of buying back, on an insurance arrangement or service level agreement, those services which they need and value, or to spend the money elsewhere. The Authority's role is to concentrate on quality and performance to ensure that excellent services are provided. The Education Department has been transformed into Somerset Education Services which is currently the LEA but is capable of becoming an independent company if necessary.

Somerset has identified service units for all aspects of activity including those units whose budgets are being devolved to schools and those which currently provide services to members, to the LEA and to individuals. Those service units whose budgets are being devolved to schools will have support in marketing, pricing, policy and financial systems. These will operate within the overall SES umbrella and have a recognizable brand image. Schools will be offered the option of an all-in provision. We should be in a key position to meet the needs of LEA schools, those who go grant maintained and others. For those services we cannot provide ourselves we shall act as broker with recognized other providers such as higher education. Those areas could include teacher training, supply and recruitment.

Somerset has adopted this approach because the Education Reform Act means that 85 per cent of the general schools budget must be devolved to schools via a formula which is largely based on pupil numbers. That general schools budget contains money which pays for services normally provided centrally for school. Schools which go GMS take 100 per cent of the budget. In pursuing the philosophy of the self-managed school, Somerset has encouraged LEA schools to look at that 15 per cent of the budget which pays for such services to see whether they wish to have the money devolved to them to buy or not buy back as they and their governors determine. It is important to remember that once funds are transferred to schools and colleges, the LEA is not precluded from providing the services the funds pay for, it simply loses its automatic right to do so. There is, however, a need to ensure that quality support services are still available for those schools and colleges which need them. For those services which the LEA no longer holds the budget, the volume of work needs to be maintained at a variable level. The move to a more sales-orientated culture does not result simply from a desire to sell as such, to be more commercial for the sake of it, but from a wish to ensure that quality support services remain available while giving schools and colleges choice.

In Somerset, our aim is for self-managing schools within an LEA context. If, however, large numbers of schools seek grant maintained status, we would want to ensure that quality services are there to support GMS schools where they want them and for the remaining, probably smaller schools which cannot easily manage without those services. Obviously there are still key Statutory functions which the LEA has to provide, such as ensuring there are sufficient school places; getting children to school and ensuring that they attend; making arrangements for children with special needs; making awards to students. The LEA must not, however, cling to the weak vine of statute but look ahead to new roles which is that of providing services to clients.

That means there is a need to create a new culture. It is a culture which can operate well within an LEA umbrella but one which could be taken elsewhere. It must be responsive, creative, listening, communicating; it must stand for good management, for realistic partnership; it must highlight and concentrate on those areas it can do well; inspection and advice to schools on the provision and management of a high quality curriculum, together with a range of expertise, personnel, health and safety, legal and financial and property issues. Those areas which others can do as well and which require new skills must be relinquished. Schools might be advised to take the same approach.

What is clear, however, is that although the National Curriculum has played an important part in bringing about these changes, it can be seen as having strengthened the role of LEAs. It is the other clauses of the 1988 Education Reform Act, relating to local management, open enrolment and grant maintained status, together with the provisions of the Local Government Act concerning compulsory competitive tendering and the 1992 Education Act for inspection, that challenge and alter fundamentally the traditional role of local education authorities.

*Chapter 8*

---

# Training for the National Curriculum

---

*Bill Lahr*

'It was the best of times, it was the worst of times. . .'. That litany of con-tradictions sums up the turmoil of all revolutions, and it is not too fanciful to apply it to the one in which we find ourselves. The National Curriculum, a revolution in itself, is beset by dissensions, uncertainty and ambiguity. There are clashes of opinion which reflect the antithesis suggested by the title of this volume. Contradictory perceptions of the National Curriculum jeopardize the many things in it which are valuable. There are those who will remain implac-ably opposed to the National Curriculum on ideological grounds, but for the majority of critics the main objection is that the agenda seems over-ambitious. They argue that it is unrealistic to hope for the delivery of the Orders as they have been conceived.

A recent major report identifies what seems to be a growing erosion of confidence in the capacity of teachers either to deliver the whole body of the National Curriculum or to come to terms with the complexities of its component parts. *Curriculum Organization and Classroom Peactice in Primary Schools*, the so-called *Three Wise Men's Report*, questions in a number of respects whether primary teachers will be able to cope with the managerial, intellectual and conceptual terms of the full range of Orders and translate them into effec-tive classroom practice. This view has been echoed in a series of regional primary seminars organized by the National Curriculum Council where teachers voiced their reservations about the capacity of the present systems of curriculum management and classroom practice at Key Stages 1 and 2 to meet the requirements of the National Curriculum. They suggested that the pace of introduction of the core and foundation subjects had been too hasty, giving insufficient time for the Orders to be properly assimilated into their planning. The curriculum was felt to be overloaded, particularly at Key Stage 2, and the teachers were concerned that the excessive amount of content, and consequent pressures upon time, would lead to selective teaching.

Criticism of this nature is supported by evidence that in many primary schools only the most tentative attempts are being made to incorporate history and geography into regular programmes of work. At the same time a majority of teachers will continue to face with trepidation the advent of Orders for physical education, music and art, with, so far, little in the way of concentrated planning to deal with these new demands.

Much of the concern currently attaching to the National Curriculum is thus focussed on Key Stages 1 and 2. It rests on doubts about primary teachers' ability to cope with the range of curriculum confronting them and to acquire the specialist knowledge and expertise they will need. It points to the problems of managing the increased and complicated demands that the new assessment arrangements will create, and the significant adjustments that will need to be made to classroom management and organization. It is suggested in some quarters that expanding curriculum demands are distracting from attention to core areas of the curriculum leading to regression in achievement and progress. Concern is also expressed about the future of small primary schools, which will face considerable difficulties in providing full curriculum coverage, in addition to the financial pressures emanating from the Government and the Audit Commission.

Such reservations are serious enough in themselves, but they are not confined to Key Stages 1 and 2. Critics cite other areas of difficulty and breakdown:

- the decision of the National Curriculum Council to advise the Secretary of State of the need for thorough revision of the Technology Order, and his response. This, despite the original claim that it is 'a radically new and exciting subject which represents a major challenge to previous understanding and practice'. The Council concludes that the programmes of study and the statements of attainment require fundamental revision to introduce more flexibility and choice, particularly at secondary level;
- the difficulty being encountered by teachers at Key Stage 2 in providing for differentiation;
- the difficulty at Key Stages 3 and 4 of tackling major cross-curricular issues; and
- the indisputable evidence of inadequate resourcing that will seriously impede progress across all the Key Stages and will probably prove fatal to the full realization of the modern languages Orders (see chapter by John Atkins).

But for all those who hold such views, and who advocate dilution, reduction or outright abolition, there is a formidable body of opinion that will fight to see the National Curriculum preserved. They believe that it represents the best attempt so far to chart the education needed by children who will grow up to be citizens of another century. They see the way in which it has been mapped as the first potentially effective attempt to tackle the complex areas of progression and continuity. They welcome the emergence of a common and unifying vocabulary about teaching and learning. They point to what has been already achieved, especially at Key Stages 1 and 2, as encouraging evidence of a grand blueprint being realized in practice, of children's learning experiences being broadened and their horizons expanded. They maintain that teachers' professional competence and confidence have been enlarged, and that there is a new awareness about curriculum issues. They testify to a growing mastery of assessment processes that is enabling teachers to focus in an analytical and more informed way on children's learning.

They point out that schools increasingly accept the necessity for corporate planning on the part of all staff, that teachers are more confident about sharing practice and working together where possible. Certainly experienced observers of schools would claim that teachers, especially at Key Stages 1 and 2, are better informed about curriculum than they have ever been.

Educationists who hold such views will not be deflected from their opinion that the National Curriculum is a powerful and valuable achievement, which though open to change and adjustment, must be maintained and developed as fully as possible.

There is clearly a considerable gap between those who view the National Curriculum as a great new opportunity and those who resist it as an imposed, unrealistic and irrelevant initiative. However, the need for in-service provision and training is one issue on which there is common agreement. Many of the severest critics accept that adequate, appropriate and sufficient in-service provision would ameliorate much of what they see as negative or unacceptable. Correspondingly, those determined to preserve the new initiative are convinced that with proper in-service support teachers will be enabled to realize for pupils all that the National Curriculum can offer.

This chapter attempts to define what seems most urgently required to support the implementation of the whole National Curriculum and to consider means and strategies for providing it.

There is a real danger that misleadingly comforting conclusions are being drawn from the acknowledgments of what teachers have achieved. Such recognition is timely; it is remarkable that so much has been accomplished, given the magnitude of the task, particularly when one recalls that in the early stages teachers were invited — by influential voices — to ignore the whole thing on the grounds that it would probably go away! To their credit, the majority of teachers and schools set about making the best of an awesome task, realizing that it was they, and not the pundits with their seductive advice, who would make or break the National Curriculum.

They were supported by a variety of agencies; by the National Curriculum Council and by the DES, by institutes of higher education and, most crucially, though in varying degrees, by local education authorities (LEAs). Despite all this, it can be argued that collective relief at what has actually been achieved has led to undue optimism about the true state of affairs — rather like shipwrecked sailors who are overjoyed at struggling to land but have not yet had time to take account of the forbidding and inhospitable nature of the landscape.

Undue pessimism is potentially as harmful as excessive optimism. It is vital, therefore, that we identify and understand where schools really are in relation to the National Curriculum.

We have already referred to the considerable advance made by teachers in terms of their professional development, their confidence and awareness about curriculum, their enhanced capacity to work together, to articulate and to share expertise. HMI and the National Curriculum Council, in their monitoring, have documented a range of positive achievements, including significant progress in connection with the core subjects and Key Stage 1. They have pointed to provision of science at the primary stage, a determined attempt to reevaluate the place and purpose of project approaches, the successful assimilation of subject changes and developments at Key Stage 3, and, across the Key Stages, a notable advance in effective assessment and recording strategies. Such developments have generated in turn serious reflection on areas of fundamental importance: on classroom management and pedagogy, on children's achievement and teacher expectation, and on the nature and significance of subjects at primary level. They have brought new emphasis on the perennial need for continuity between phases of education, from home to the very end of statutory schooling.

All this is highly encouraging, but its promise will be fulfilled only if we are realistic about what remains to be achieved. The evidence from surveys by HMI, the National Curriculum Council, the professional associations and various research bodies is unlikely to be providing a wholly accurate account of the true situation, if only because it is already out of date. Perhaps the most interesting indicator of this is the apparently sudden realization that the technology Orders have encountered such difficulties. Suggestions of unease about this area of the curriculum have been emerging for some time, like sudden shudders on the surface of a mill pond, but it has been all too easy to ignore them in an atmosphere amounting almost to complacency.

There has been a wide variety of training provided by a range of agencies, which have included LEAs, institutions of higher education, the National Curriculum Council, professional associations and groups, professional training and consultants and schools. With such a wide diversity, standards are bound to vary: perhaps this is occurring to an unacceptable degree from LEA to LEA. Some have made comprehensive and well resourced training available, while others have responded inconsistently. In many cases, provision has been made for the core areas of the National Curriculum, to some extent for technology, but has not gone beyond that in any systematic way.

In some cases the increasingly discredited cascade model has been the preferred mode, with consequent loss in coherence and clarity. The success of some training has been dependent upon the goodwill of teachers and their readiness to attend twilight sessions, when they can be at their least energetic and receptive.

Changes in funding have had major repercussions on the provision LEAs are able to make, especially in relation to subject training, obliged as they are to choose between advisory teacher provision or direct training activities. In many subject areas it is no longer possible for advisory teachers to be employed at all, at a time when the changing role of advisory services within the LEAs prevent them from undertaking in-service training and development work in specific subject areas. Without any alternatives on offer, this is a worrying state of affairs.

English, mathematics and science, and, until recently, technology, have begun to be taken almost for granted as being satisfactorily addressed in schools. Yet the evidence is that there is still substantial need for training in these areas, especially at Key Stage 2, but at Key Stage 1 as well. The widely valued twenty day courses for mathematics and science are, of course, available, but they can address the needs of a relatively small number of teachers in any given authority each year. Training for English may be particularly vulnerable. There is an understandable tendency in teachers, and especially primary teachers, to make assumptions about their personal expertise in English which may not be justified. Teachers are more ready to acknowledge their insecurities in technology, history and geography, particularly at Key Stage 2, and the trepidation with which they anticipate the Orders for music, art and physical education. Despite the training input both nationally and locally, we have not begun to do more than scratch the surface of current needs in relation to individual subject areas. Even where teachers have a confident subject grasp, they face the considerable challenge of ensuring effective differentiation.

Major areas which appear to require substantial in-service provision and training are:

- The development and extension of individual subject expertise, especially at Key Stages 1 and 2, but also at Key Stage 3, where, for example, in science and modern languages new curriculum demands require a reappraisal not merely of methodology but also of content. They would appear to demand that courses based on the twenty day model be provided.
- Classroom management, especially in relation to provision for differentiation.
- Management and recording of assessment.
- Management of the provision of cross-curricular elements, especially at Key Stages 3 and 4.
- Management of whole curriculum and staff development.

The last of these is critical to the achievement of effective in-service and training. Much depends upon the management skills of senior and middle status leaders in terms of inspiration, curriculum analysis and monitoring. What is initiated must be systematically evaluated and followed up with practical support.

*The Three Wise Men* Report says of effective headteachers that they

... have a vision of what their schools should become. They will seek to establish this vision through the development of shared educational beliefs which underpin evaluative judgments, school policies and decision-making generally. The vision will have at its heart a clearly articulated view of what constitutes the school curriculum including, very importantly, its relationship to the National Curriculum (and of how planning, teaching and evaluations will be undertaken in order to ensure that the aims and objectives of the curriculum are translated into pupil learning).

It might be added that this applies equally to other senior staff responsible for staff development, and for curriculum leadership. The difference will be one only of degree.

There has been a growing assumption that training which was increasingly based in and focussed upon schools would be more likely to be successful than that externally provided. This assumption is probably based on an over-optimistic view of what teachers can achieve when brought together within the context of their own institution. The fact is, as we have become increasingly aware, that INSET provision is a complicated art not acquired overnight. It requires more than goodwill and the reassurance of a familiar context and colleagues who daily share it. INSET providers require as much training as their consumers.

It may be useful at this point to remind ourselves of some of the acknowledged truths in relation to the provision of productive INSET. This has been authoritatively defined as:

> ... the development of the individual which arises from the whole range of events and activities by which serving teachers can extend their personal academic or practical education, their professional competence and their understanding of educational principles and methods. (Stephens, 1975)

Subsequently there has been a growing recognition that provision would be more effective where it addressed the needs of the individual member of a professional community in the broader context of the corporate needs of schools themselves. A helpful distinction has been drawn for us between training and in-service:

> ... training is concerned with the acquisition of skills and techniques, using standardised learning procedures and sequences. ... In contrast the broader conception of in-service education is bound up with the notion of bringing about professional, academic and personal development to the provision of a whole series of study experiences and activities of which training should be viewed as but one aspect. (Morant)

Successful INSET demands certain prerequisites, apart from being closely related to needs. Learning is likely to be more effective:

(i)   Where opportunities are created for peer-based interaction which encourages reflection, analysis and solution of problems through shared effort.

(ii)  Where there are opportunities to 'ground' theory in practice through experiment and shared experience, including visits to other schools.

(iii) Where inputs are interspersed with practical assignments, and time is given to absorb and assimilate. There must be feedback information to improve and shape INSET to meet need, and above all support in follow-up, which Fullan has defined as crucial to successful staff training and development because 'it is continuous and developmental: it is concrete, relevant and keyed to specific needs, it is integrated with processes of monitoring, evaluation and the creation of materials; it is designed to change the way people relate to each other and work together; it uses demonstration, observation and practice'.

The tendency to place total confidence in the efficacy of school-based in-service, even to the exclusion of external agencies and influences, may have been over-optimistic. Danger of 'a recycling of inadequacies' and the fact that in some cases 'they may not know what they do not know' has encouraged a return to a mixed economy. This has received a powerful impetus from the work of people like Professor Robin Alexander who have stressed the importance of developing a continuum of professional development and training based on a sequence of initial teacher training, professional induction and sequential professional development.

Individually and collectively these factors are critically important to the success of in-service provision. There is no doubt that many INSET initiatives and projects — inventive, creative, even grandiose — have sunk without trace or had little lasting impact, even where they have been carefully thought through. It is equally certain that some, if not all, of the factors referred to above will be found to have been absent.

There are those who find it incongruous that a National Curriculum intended to remove the element of lottery that still attaches to many children's education, dependent upon where they live or economic or other circumstances, should suffer in turn from a *laissez-faire* approach to training. They believe that national requirements and developments must be matched by national provision that would entitle all teachers to a minimum INSET/training allowance. This, they suggest, might be comprised of:

(i)   core mandatory components relating to classroom management, differentiated learning, assessment and record keeping, cross-curricular provision, special needs, and the teaching of literacy and numeracy; and

(ii)   training for all in specific subject areas.

Funding would be arranged to secure cooperation between small authorities and the involvement of teacher training institutions with LEAs. In the light of current needs, such provision should be made as a matter of urgency, perhaps over a period of a week, added to one of the normal half-terms. Many, in addition, feel that the current arrangements for five training days should be permanently extended by at least one day, with schools required to provide specific elements as described above as part of their programme.

Proposals of this nature raise the issue of resources. One of the most remarkable aspects of the Education Reform Act has been the relatively calm acceptance by the teaching profession of the central Government's assumption that the revolutionary reforms required in education would be achieved with minimal extra funding. Even the most sceptical may be convinced by reference to the study commissioned by the National Union of Teachers into the likely cost of implementation that the Government estimates are extraordinarily naive or desperately parsimonious (see chapter 9).

Should the Government maintain such a stance, then proposals of the kind set out in this chapter would be unlikely to materialize. The amount of funding currently provided through GEST is in itself insufficient to provide adequate training for a basic curriculum. What has been done so far has been achieved to a substantial extent by the provision of supplementary funding by local education authorities, with supply time to allow for teacher release and support for development through the use of advisory teachers. This is rapidly breaking down as increased delegation makes it impossible for LEAs to continue supplementing GEST funding.

Delegation has serious implications for training. Experience from both education and industry suggests that schools may not choose to make from the delegated budgets sufficient provision for training and development. The available evidence indicates that additional funding is put into staffing, and that training allowances are the first to suffer where there is financial shortfall — it is the British disease. There seems therefore no escaping from the fact that if National Curriculum training is to be effective, then funding has not only to be provided in a way that will ensure provision at institutional level, but that it has to be precisely earmarked.

It may no longer be practical, or perhaps even desirable, to continue with advisory teachers, although they ranked, at their best, among the most successful elements in effective in-service. A promising alternative is available in terms of limited secondment by local education authorities in conjunction with their schools. These secondments, offered to headteachers, to senior teachers and to staff with particular expertise, would not extend beyond a half-term and could well achieve what was required within a period as short as a fortnight or a month. Teachers would be seconded in small groups for specific tasks. Two such group secondments have recently taken place in the City of Westminster, where small groups of teachers and headteachers have been freed from their schools, with supply cover provided, to enable them to consider in a concentrated way the production of exemplar materials in connection with early years education and the place of project approaches at Key Stages 1 and 2. These groups have visited other authorities, acquiring materials to enable them to produce working documents that focus on policy and practical implementation in the classrooms. These will be marketed nationally.

The limitations of this initiative will be obvious: it is local, it has a severe time constraint, it is likely to be utilitarian, and the limitation on group size necessarily reduces the range of expertise. Such groups would benefit from the support of an outside consultant, with a large theoretical and practical background. Such initiatives might be developed nationally on a wider scale, with a body such as the National Curriculum Council as sponsor.

Consider a particular example. The more one views practice across the Key Stages the clearer it seems that the National Curriculum would be made more feasible in terms of implementation by the production of effective schemes of work. They are called for throughout the National Curriculum Orders and literature, and are referred to in HMI reports as if they were a common place. The reverse is nearer the truth, especially at primary level where there is still a tendency for teachers to regard schemes of work as confined within single subject bounds and therefore likely to be restrictive in terms of cross-curricular work. As a consequence, the mere definition of a scheme of work becomes difficult.

Working groups commissioned to develop scheme exemplars might produce materials that would serve, at least, as starting points for individuals or whole staffs. Such groups would work on a wide range of issues, producing guidelines, devising strategies and designing materials. Where materials became marketable to a wider audience, then the designers would become eligible for a share in subsequent financial profit.

What then of advisory teachers? They have played a prominent role in in-service over the last decade and have generated almost as much controversy. They have been criticized by professional associations and teacher bodies as peripheral to the demanding and urgent business of classrooms, and often by education committees as an expensive indulgence likely to propagate idiosyncratic, permissive and undemanding approaches. Partly as a consequence of this they have almost vanished from the scene. Yet the criticism has not quite obscured their potential value and the extent to which they can enable teachers to extend and enhance personal performance in favourable circumstances. Many schools still value their particular expertise, knowledge of a wide range of developments in different contexts, and the ability to intervene in practically supportive ways. They believe that a force teaching in their 'home' schools for the major proportion of their time, but seconded out for a day or two each week for advisory purposes, would be in a position to bring their expertise to INSET while at the same time avoiding difficulties such as 'classroom re-entry' that the old model generated.

Research indicates that where schools have choice they will continue to purchase advisory teachers to 'work alongside' teachers in classroom contexts. There is no doubt that particular projects (for example the work of the Literacy Development Teams in Hackney in the 80s) have produced visible gains in children's performance. Against that there is the danger of a dependency model that does not sustain development when the class teacher is 'isolated' again. The most effective model seems to be an advisory teacher working together with change 'agents' such as heads of departments drawn from a consortium of neighbouring institutions.

Many of these proposals presuppose the involvement of the LEA either as inspirer, mediator or maintainer. If they are not to be so, then one way forward must be through competitive bidding. Funding would be devolved to regional or local funding councils and the model, a development of the Technology Initiative, would encourage groups of schools (consortia), perhaps in some cases combinations of primary and secondary, to set up development projects. An example might be a project to develop curriculum materials for geography in years 6 and 7.

The funding would be sufficient to allow for the employment of consultancy support. Performance indicators, more vigorous and specific than those associated with GEST, would be employed, specific to the project as well as consonant with national priorities. They would be monitored by the funding agency using a bought-in inspection agency.

Related to such development, and indeed to in-service and training in its wider sense is the issue of teacher accreditation. At present, apart from what is known as job satisfaction, there seems to be insufficient incentives for teachers to take further their own professional growth. Indeed, that so many continue to seek training is a testament to their commitment. Many HE providers offer forms of accreditation for teacher training and development. However, this often allows them to extract a high price for nominal accreditation; that is the actual work is done by the teacher involved, often in conjunction with a local advisory service. The institution simply accredits and charges what is often a high fee for the service.

This monopoly on accreditation needs to be challenged. It might be done in two ways: the notion of a record of achievement for teachers, the increasing use of NVQ to accredit teachers' work and the ensuring of transferability between NVQ and locally accredited schemes and higher degrees.

The national Curriculum has something of the stuff of epic about it. In the best epic tradition, the great and the good took up opposing views. Half-forgotten divisions were revived and old vendettas renewed.

They set out together, the ardent with the most unwilling, but all, in the end, determined, now that the voyage was engaged on, to make the best of it. And at first things went well, despite the gloomy prophecies of false charts, of inadequate provision, of rumours that the land for which they sailed really did not exist at all. The most humble of all the participants in the great design, the Lower Deck Rowers, covered themselves with glory by their commitment to the task and their determination not to give in. Even the most exalted of the leaders and the designers regarded their efforts with gratitude and as an omen of final success.

But inevitable storm clouds gathered and vicissitudes befell them. The Rowers on the second deck found the oars more unwieldly and technically difficult to manoeuvre.

The enterprise at the moment is in a situation more perilous perhaps than we have realized. It is caused essentially by a lack of nerve, by a wish on the part of some to turn back to a safer landfall, which though not the sought-for destination, can be regarded at least as some kind of progress.

Whatever becomes of the original plan, there can be no gainsaying the vital importance of in-service and training that is generous, that responds to clearly-defined needs, that takes account of experience to date of teachers and those who have monitored the National Curriculum, and takes some regard of the measures proposed here.

*Part 4*

# Perspectives on the Future

*Chapter 9*

# Resourcing the National Curriculum

*John Atkins*

## Introduction

Previous chapters have explored the background to the National Curriculum and its theoretical impact on school curricula. However, the implementation of education innovation is usually characterized by uncertainty over its real cost in practice, and the consequent effect on other education activity.

On the one hand, implementation of the National Curriculum might be a straightforward, easy to resource exercise in substituting a national set of curriculum guidelines for a local one. On the other hand, implementation could place demands on the resources of schools, human and financial, that they were quite unable to meet. They could come close to failing — or be driven to failure elsewhere in the system. Only by assessing the cost of the curriculum innovation concerned can a balance be struck.

Although education researchers often focus on the progress of curricular innovations, taking time to study the human and financial resource costs of these is by no means universal. Certainly such studies are difficult to carry out, for a number of reasons. First, no curriculum innovation takes place against a background of no other change. The wide-reaching nature of the National Curriculum legislation will have placed it at the head of most schools' action lists; but the relatively long duration of change — nine years at least from the start of Key Stage 1 mathematics implementation to the end of Key Stage 4 music — has meant that many other changes have been introduced or will be introduced along the way.

While the National Curriculum has been in progress, schools have had to cope, *inter alia*, with the introduction of Local Management of Schools (LMS), the last stages of implementation of the General Certificate of Secondary Education (GCSE), new approaches to teacher appraisal and a new strategy and structure for school development planning. Even when a defined change has taken place in school or classroom organization, it is often unreasonable to ask the school concerned to disentangle the reasons for change and distribute them across this list.

The human and financial resource cost of change depends critically on the extent of human and financial resources available. Bluntly, if asked to implement a change on the basis of virtually no extra resources, most well-disposed people will try to do so. If asked to draw up in advance a list of the costs of a change, all but the most unworldly will take the opportunity to resource the new arrangements at a higher level than formerly. Neither picture of change costs will be a fair one.

It is far from easy, therefore, to identify the extra costs associated with the implementation of the National Curriculum, if these costs are defined by comparison with 'what would have been spent anyway'. Yet this is the only basis for calculation.

Despite these reservations, a number of organizations believed the extent of change caused by National Curriculum implementation to be so great that an assessment of the costs of implementation would be worthwhile. In particular, the National Union of Teachers commissioned Coopers & Lybrand to carry out two separate studies of the costs of implementing the National Curriculum (in primary and secondary schools respectively during the autumn term of 1991). This chapter draws on these studies.[1]

## The Background to the Research

Before discussing our findings in detail, a number of reservations should be made. These reservations stem in part from the conceptual difficulties described above and in part from the small sample size inevitable if individual schools are to be studied in sufficient depth.

To achieve this depth, our project was based on a case study methodology. The conclusions are therefore not straight 'averages' across the schools in our sample, but represent our best judgment between the two extremes of 'no funding' and 'as much as you would like' described above. As such, they are — like all professional judgments — open to question; but we have sought to make a reasonable, rather than an extreme, assessment of implementation costs.

## Types of Cost

There are two ways in which the costs involved in National Curriculum implementation can be classified. First, costs, can be *direct* costs or *opportunity* costs: the former are costs that can be immediately identified in financial terms, while the latter are the implied costs incurred when one activity (or 'opportunity') is foregone in order to devote time and resources to another. An example, drawn from primary schools, might be less time spent on listening to reading in order to spend more time on the 'new' National Curriculum subjects — i.e. science, technology, history and geography. Converting opportunity costs into money terms requires some assessment of the 'value' of the activities foregone: this is what makes their identification problematic. The second cost classification is between *start-up* costs, which (although they may run for some years) represent the one-off costs of conversion from an old system to the new, and *recurrent* costs which are likely to be incurred indefinitely on a regular basis.

These two cost distinctions form a matrix, with individual costs being classified as direct startup, direct recurrent, opportunity-startup, or opportunity recurrent as appropriate. All the costs we quote below are at November 1991 prices.

## The Primary School Study

Our first study was based on questionnaires and interviews at twenty-five primary schools in five different local authorities in England and Wales.

### Direct Costs: Teaching Staff

In the schools we surveyed, the highest direct cost identified by heads was the cost of extra staffing needed to address the requirements of assessment. In our view, this amounted to the equivalent of one FTE teacher in a school of 200. Heads also saw the need for extra incentive allowances to enable them to support curriculum development in the 'new' subjects — ideally two scale 'A' allowances in a 200-place school. At the same time, existing allowances were being diverted away from cross-curricular responsibilities (pastoral care, special needs support) towards other specific National Curriculum subjects.

This drive towards subject-based incentive allowances reflects the increasing specialization of the primary school curriculum. Although heads we spoke to were still adamant in avoiding the model of the 'primary science teacher' who taught nothing else, they were starting to recognize the importance of allocating specialisms through an otherwise generalist staff.

Taken together, the extra teaching post and two extra allowances represent a direct recurrent cost of £107.25 per pupil per year.[2]

Interestingly, none of the schools had attempted to reduce class size in order to cope with the demands of the National Curriculum. Indeed, we identified an occasional tendency under LMS to let class sizes increase in order to recover resources elsewhere.

### Other Direct Costs

As might be expected, given the large share that staff costs make up of any school's budget, the other identified costs of National Curriculum implementation did not approach the cost of extra staffing. However, schools did identify some significant costs in a number of areas.

The major additional costs were for books and teaching resources. With the exception of a few, very well resourced schools, most schools anticipated substantial increases in expenditure on material directly related to National Curriculum subjects and programmes of study. We model this increase expenditure as £10 per pupil over the years — £30 start-up expenditure in total.

Neither we nor the schools are able to identify whether maintaining stocks of National Curriculum learning materials would be any more expensive; we do not therefore include any extra recurrent costs in our model.

Almost all schools envisaged extra spending on equipment. Our model figure — £4.50 per pupil per year for five years, or £22.50 start-up in total — may seem low. However, this is a key area where what schools have to spend appears directly to govern their assessment of need; put another way, almost any level of spending on equipment (whether National Curriculum or not) can be justified if there are the resources freely available.

Again we were unable to identify any long-term recurrent costs.

Around half the schools we studied anticipated extra expenditure on consumables and expenses (photocopying, postage, etc). The amounts were small, and we use a figure of £2 per pupil per year recurrent for our model.

Finally, we allow for a miscellaneous start-up expenditure of £5.20 per pupil over two years (£3.85 in the first year) to cover minor premises refurbishment, provision of extra storage space for pupils' work (important for ongoing assessment), etc.

## Total Direct Costs

Taken together, these staff and non-staff costs amount to direct recurrent costs of £109.25 per year, and direct start-up costs of £57.70. Both these figures are per pupil. On the basis of a current UK primary school population of around four million these figures represent direct recurrent costs of £437m and direct start-up costs of £231m.

For comparison, £109.25 per pupil per year represents around 6 per cent of a school's recurrent budget.

## Opportunity Costs

First, we expected (and found) a number of shifts in the balance of the primary curriculum, led by the increased emphasis being placed on the 'new' primary school subjects. Thus almost all schools reported increases in time spent on science and technology (around two-and-a-half hours per week) and on history and geography (around one-and-a-half hours per week between them). These increases were met from reductions in English and mathematics, together with reductions in time spent in the first years listening to children read.

It may seem perverse to meet these increases from the core National Curriculum subjects. However, the scale of the increases required (four hours represents towards 20 per cent or one day of the teaching week) meant that English and maths were bound to suffer.

Of greater concern is the reduction in time spent listening to children read. In part this reflects a shift away from individual activities towards more class-based activities in order to 'get through' the National Curriculum content. Whether this represents an improvement will remain to be seen. There is pressure from some quarters for more whole class teaching for more doctrinaire reasons.

These shifts in curriculum balance are, we believe, ongoing rather than for one or two years only. Whether they represent an opportunity *cost* of the National Curriculum, or indeed represent an improvement, must be an educational judgment; and we do not include figures for them in our model.

We do, however, include figures in the model related to the increase in teachers' 'activities other than teaching'. Such activities may fall in school time or in teachers' own time out of school; and increases in these activities represent opportunity costs either of school, activities foregone or of leisure time lost. We observed increases in time spent training, in staff meetings, in preparing information for parents, and in other curriculum maintenance activities associated with the National Curriculum. Staff were also spending more time covering for absent colleagues (usually away on training); under LMS, schools could be reluctant to spend money on 'supply cover' which they could instead spend on books, equipment, etc.

In our model, we assess the extra amount of time spent at present by teachers on these activities as amounting to seventeen days per teacher in school time and nineteen in teachers' own time. To model what will be a slow but significant reduction in the time for these activities as teachers gain familiarity with the tasks concerned, we assume these levels will remain for three further years and then will decrease to just under six and ten days respectively.

In order to cost these inputs, we assume that the value of activities foregone is equivalent to the teachers' salaries for the time concerned (on a 190 day teaching year basis). Allowing eight teachers (plus head) for our 200-pupil school leads to opportunity costs of around £144.50 per pupil per year for the first three years and £58.50 thereafter.[3]

What this analysis conceals, of course, is the cost of this extra workload — particularly the out-of-school workload — in stress terms. Nineteen days' extra work outside school time represents around one day extra per fortnight — one Saturday in two, for example, on top of the load which many teachers already carry outside school hours. Although the 'costs of stress' are not as easily quantifiable as the other costs we have identified, the effect on teachers' lives of this extra load must be considerable.

*Summary of Primary Costs*

Putting together the analyses of direct and opportunity costs identified above, our model calculates the total recurrent cost per primary school pupil of National Curriculum implementation as just under £168 per pupil per year, with start-up costs over the first two, three or four years totalling just under a further £316. On the same basis as before, this suggests a total recurrent cost of £671m and a start-up cost of £1,262m across England and Wales.

## The Secondary School Study

Given the relatively greater complexity of secondary schools, our secondary survey of the costs of National Curriculum implementation followed a more explicit case study model. Seven schools, in the same five local education authorities, as in the primary study were investigated in detail during extended visits. Similar headings to those described for primary schools were used to identify costs.

Due to the uncertainty still surrounding Key Stage 4, we restrict our curriculum cost model to Key Stage 3 and its effects.

*Direct Costs: Teaching Staff*

Again, the major direct impact of National Curriculum implementation on secondary schools was in staff costs.

As in primary schools, the National Curriculum is changing the balance of the curriculum towards some subjects and away from others. In the secondary schools we surveyed, the 'gainer' subjects were science, technology and modern foreign languages. The 'loser' subjects varied from school to school.

Of itself, a shift in time allocation between subjects does not incur extra costs. However, since secondary teachers do not as a rule teach more than one subject, a shift in time allocation can lead to a temporary staffing imbalance. We make a small allowance for this imbalance in our model (equivalent to 0.5 FTE teachers in a school of 800) for one year only. (This represents £11.65 per pupil.[4])

Unlike primary schools, however, some of our secondary schools had acted to reduce class size — though not all, and not by much. We make a similar allowance, equivalent to 0.5 FTE per year recurrent, to reflect this. (Again this represents £11.65 per pupil per year.)

By far the largest cost, however, is concerned with assessment and the staff meetings related to assessments. As in our primary school survey, the assessment requirements of the National Curriculum were seen as making significant extra demands of staff time in the secondary schools of our sample. Our judgment is that even in the long term the equivalent of four periods (typically 140 minutes) per teacher per week will be needed. From comments made in the case study schools, we expect half of this to be met by direct funding and half as an opportunity cost from other school activities or teachers' own time.

Again, as with the primary schools, we anticipate a higher level of activity in the first few years of Key Stage 3 implementation as teachers develop assessment materials. We allow as much time again for the first three years of implementation (which will of course vary from subject to subject). This makes a total of 280 minutes per week in these three years, again half met by extra staffing in our model and half as an opportunity cost.

In our typical 800-place school, this extra time represents 11 FTE staff for the first three years and 5.5 FTE staff thereafter, with half of each figure being direct cost as already stated. (This direct cost represents £129.50 per pupil in the first three years and £64.75 thereafter.)

Secondary schools were also able to identify specific time needs for curriculum development, which we model at the equivalent of one extra FTE teacher for two years. (This represents two periods per week for one-third of the staff in the school at any one time, and costs £23.31 per pupil for each year.)

Since secondary schools already have a subject-based incentive allowance structure, National Curriculum implementation was not seen as requiring further subject-based incentive allowances in the case study schools. Instead, in a reversal of the primary approach, these secondary schools sought to create one or two new *cross-curricular* posts of responsibility, sometimes reflecting specific National Curriculum cross-curricular themes. Our model includes two-and-a-half additional scale 'A' allowances for our model 800-place school, at a cost per pupil of £4.37 per year recurrent.

Again, unlike primary schools, secondary schools had made more direct provision for staff cover for in-service training. The provision was moderate, however, and our model includes only sufficient to provide three days' staff cover per four teachers per year (£6.09 per pupil per year).

The direct teaching staff costs above amount to £86.86 recurrent per pupil per year, with start-up costs of £252.52 per pupil over the first three years.

### Direct Costs: Non-teaching Staff

Secondary schools identified an increased demand for technician support to reflect increases in time spent on technology, science and IT, and the spread of complex equipment within these subjects. Schools also predicted extra clerical staff needs linked to record keeping for assessment. Our model includes a modest provision of £10,000 per school per year (£12.50 per pupil) to buy in extra technician and clerical staffing.

*Other Direct Costs*

The other direct costs we identified were similar in scope to those identified in primary schools (although the secondary work covered Key Stage 3 only). Additional direct start-up costs for books and teaching resources (including library provision) are modelled at £32.60 per pupil over three or four years, and again no recurrent consequences could be identified.

Extra spending on equipment is modelled at £53.75 per pupil in total over three years (compare the primary figure of £22.50). This increase may in part reflect greater expectations on equipment spend in the secondary sector. In our responses, however, it was specifically tied to considerable extra investment in information technology which secondary schools, but not yet primary schools, recognized as an overriding need. The secondary schools were also able to identify some recurrent cost consequences of maintaining this new equipment: £5 per pupil per year.

Secondary schools, like primary schools, anticipated an extra recurrent spend on consumables largely to reflect National Curriculum assessment costs. Our model allows £3.70 per pupil per year.

The final direct cost category is a contrast with our primary survey. Secondary schools identified significant needs for premises refurbishment (usually related to increasing science or technology space) to meet National Curriculum demands, and our model allows for a one-off amount of £37.50 per pupil to pay for it. Again the contrast between secondary and primary schools is probably, in part, one of expectation of spend. However, it has been suggested to us that some primary schools are in such need of refurbishment in any case that to try to relate specific refurbishment requirements to National Curriculum demands is impossible.

*Total Direct Costs*

Taken together, these direct staff and non-staff costs amount to £108.06 per year recurrent and £376.37 start-up per pupil. For comparison, this recurrent cost represents around 6 per cent of a typical school budget.

On the basis of a secondary pupil population of 2,800,000 pupils, these cost figures represent recurrent costs of £303m per year and start-up costs of £1,054m.

*Opportunity Costs*

Our analysis of opportunity costs for secondary schools followed much the same pattern as for the earlier, primary sample. Again, we found curriculum shifts (already described) towards science and technology, joined in this instance by modern foreign languages; again, we refrain from making any educational judgment about whether this represents an opportunity *cost* of National Curriculum implementation.

As in the primary survey, the more directly teacher-related opportunity costs revolved around increases in 'activities other than teaching': assessment, meetings, curriculum development. As already mentioned, our model allows for four periods (140 minutes) per teacher week in the long term for this activity, with up to double this amount in the first three years; half of this will be at an opportunity cost to other activities.

This opportunity cost represents £129.50 per pupil in the first three years and £64.75 thereafter, equivalent of a recurrent cost of £64.75 and start-up cost of £194.25 over three years.

### Summary of Secondary Costs

Again, putting together the analyses of direct and opportunity costs identified above, our model calculates the total recurrent cost per secondary school pupil of National Curriculum implementation as just under £173 per year, with start-up costs over the first two, three or four years totalling just over a further £570. On the same basis as before, this suggests a total recurrent cost of £484m and a start-up cost of £1,598m.

## Some Conclusions

The projects to which this chapter relates were concerned to evaluate to costs which schools have incurred in implementing the National Curriculum to date, and those anticipated for the immediate future. We did not seek to evaluate whether the necessary resources were available, nor how they could be found.

But we can draw some conclusions which go beyond the detailed cost data itself. First, we are convinced that the resource cost of education innovation can be assessed, at least indicatively, despite the reservations expressed at the beginning of this chapter. The ideal would be to be able to predict the cost of innovation in advance; but this is highly difficult and likely to remain so. Being able to track the cost of an innovation in progress will at least help to ensure that innovations do not unwittingly draw resources from other school activities which cannot afford to lose them.

Secondly, our work starts to indicate some of the relationships between the direct cost contributions to curriculum innovation, which are relatively straightforward to identify, and the relatively undefined investment in opportunity costs which support the innovation itself. In a perfect funding regime, some of these opportunity costs should perhaps be converted into direct costs — for example by the employment of extra teachers. Until that time, our work demonstrates again the extent to which curriculum innovations rely, and continue to rely, on considerable effort from teaching and non-teaching staff beyond the official school day if they are to be successful.

## Notes

1 *Costs of the National Curriculum in Primary Schools*, Commissioned by NUT, Coopers and Lybrand, November 1991; and *Costs of the National Curriculum in Secondary Schools: Seven Case Studies*, Commissioned by NUT, Coopers and Lybrand, March 1992.
2 Based on nominal but realistic teachers' salaries and pupil-teacher ratios.
3 This is (clearly) an oversimplification, designed to recognize a gradual reduction in the amount of extra time needed as teachers gain familiarity with the National Curriculum.
4 Average over *all* pupils, for ease of reference.

## References

COSTS OF THE NATIONAL CURRICULUM IN SECONDARY SCHOOLS: SEVEN CASE STUDIES (1992) Commissioned by the NUT, Coopers and Lybrand.
CURRICULUM IN PRIMARY SCHOOLS (1991) Commissioned by the NUT, Coopers and Lybrand.

*Chapter 10*

# From an Entitlement to an Empowerment Curriculum

*Stewart Ranson*

## Introduction

The National Curriculum is the most significant piece of national planning in education since 1944. It will not be fully established until the year 2000, when the first cohort will have experienced every key stage of learning. The process of evaluation cannot be postponed until then; both the process of implementation, and the organizing principles need critical analysis.

The rationale of the National Curriculum has been to raise standards of attainment by: providing all pupils with the same curriculum opportunities; prescribing the structure of subjects that make up the curriculum; setting clear objectives for what children of all abilities should achieve; insisting upon careful planning and assessment of progress in learning; and improving communication with parents so that they can know what is being achieved and what is to be done. Standards, entitlement and the transmission of the nation's culture provide the guiding framework of values. Such objectives would be carefully monitored and regulated by the Department of Education and Science (now the Department for Education), supported by the National Curriculum Council. This national framework could, it was believed, secure the best of the professionally-led tradition from the 1960s, with teachers striving to respond to need and to equalize opportunities, while preventing inconsistency and fragmentation in the learning experience of young people across the country.

Some evidence has begun to emerge from HMI as well as the National Curriculum Council's monitoring reports. This shows the considerable commitment that teachers and schools have invested in the National Curriculum, which in turn has had 'a positive influence on curriculum planning in most schools, helping to foster both longer term strategy and shorter term preparations related in particular to work in the core subjects' (HMI, 1990). Many issues remain: the relationship of schemes of work to attainment targets; the dissemination of good classroom strategies; the achievement of good assessment and record-keeping; and most significantly the clarification of the relationship between national prescription and local innovation.

In this chapter, while acknowledging the achievement of the National Curriculum, I argue that if the objective is preparing 'pupils for the opportunities, responsibilities and experiences of adult life' (Section 2, Education Reform Act, 1988), then the *processes* of developing the curriculum will need to be adapted to strengthen the contribution of the local partners (LEAs, governors, teachers, parents and the community). More significantly, the *purposes* themselves will need to be redirected from entitlement to empowerment. Though entitlement and rational planning are essential conditions for reform, they are not enough because they do not reach the source of the problem of underachievement in education — the corroded springs of motivation which lie in school and society. Drawing upon recent studies of LEAs,[1] I shall consider how reform of the process and purpose of the National Curriculum can build upon its achievements and prepare more effectively for the learning society.

| Curriculum | From the 1960s | Late 1980s | Towards 2000 |
|---|---|---|---|
| **Principles** | Child-centred curriculum | The National Curriculum | An empowerment curriculum |
| **Values** | Opportunity | Entitlement | Citizenship in the learning society |
| **Purpose** | Pupil need | Prescribed subjects/themes | Active learning through practical reason |
| **Organization** | Decentralized; professional | Centralized; state | Democratic; public |
| **Power** | Teachers | Political/ administrative | Partnership |

### Managing the Process of Implementation: A County's Experience

This county LEA perceived the challenge for management as one of assimilating the national reforms while retaining a distinctive vision about the process of education within the county. Senior officers and inspectors approached the National Curriculum positively:

> We have not found significant difficulties in working with the NC — for example in English, if you unpack it, all you want to do is there. It

does not preclude the practices we want to advocate. Although we are not sure about the technology or history reports, we find maths, science and English all helpful.

Yet, although they believed that the National Curriculum often provided useful frameworks for planning, they were also clear that they needed enhancing and developing locally if they were to work effectively — 'we are not merely implementing the National Curriculum, we are about mediating and interpreting it to meet the needs of young people in the county'. Quality in teaching and learning will only be achieved by responding to the way children learn and by using the National Curriculum more as a set of guidelines, than as a straightjacket.

The county has, therefore, been creating a clear understanding of what is valued locally in teaching and learning and formulating appropriate policies for governors, teachers and parents.

The county view of quality focuses on programmes of study rather than attainment targets. (We are concerned that teachers may focus on what is to be tested and work back to what is to be studied.) We are child centred. We see education as a process of 'drawing out' as well as 'putting in'. We do think children learn best when:

- doing not merely memorizing
- learning through first hand experience
- encouraged to use their imagination
- encouraged to experiment with a variety of responses
- allowed time to produce work of quality and depth
- engaged 'actively' in their learning
- they exercise choice in learning
- they take responsibility for their learning.

Such a process places the emphasis upon children learning rather than teachers teaching. These values lead us to look at the worrying things in past practice: an over-reliance on published schemes of work; too much front of class teaching; too much closed learning — that is, children being asked questions that imply 'right' or 'wrong' answers with too little exploration, speculation and diversity of inquiry. There has, moreover, been too little opportunity for group work and discussion, and too much emphasis on pupils working alone. Good practice involves group work to plan, challenge, support, help and amplify the learning process. This does not mean that group work is a panacea — a 'best thing since sliced bread'. But it frequently is undervalued as a learning strategy. We find that good teachers use a range of methods as appropriate: individual, pair, group and whole class, according to the nature of the activity. Excessive reliance on any of these denies learning opportunities to children.

There is both a belief that a distinctive philosophy of what consitutes good education is emerging in the county and that shared agreement amongst the partners about the purposes and processes of learning is essential to quality in teaching and learning.

- Education is centrally concerned with the development of the whole child.
- All children are of equal worth and deserve equal opportunities.
- However, children are different and their needs show considerable divergence.
- Thus, effective classroom practice starts with the needs of individual children.
- Continuity and progression should be ensured for each child.
- High expectations of children.
- Close consultation with parents is essential, based on a recognition of them as prime educators in their own right.

Initially, it was felt that teachers, especially in primary schools, were unhappy at the prospect of the National Curriculum:

... there was resentment against an imposed curriculum when the experience of teachers was of parents expressing appreciation and admiration. More subtly, teachers resented the eroding of what was seen as a traditional part of their professionalism: that is, making decisions about the nature and process of learning. So initially, the National Curriculum was not popular. But the working party reports, especially the TGAT report and the statutory Orders, reassured teachers and commanded a measure of support in schools, while the National Curriculum Council had been seen to stand up against political pressure to impose a narrow grammar school curriculum.

Although the description of the curriculum was often not helpful, and they would have preferred HMI's focus upon 'areas of experience', advisers, nevertheless, came to understand that there was much overlap between the National Curriculum and county policy.

... we developed the view that the National Curriculum can be integrated with good practice in the county and enhance it; because we have been culpable of not carefully enough planning, monitoring and recording what is being learned. This can be enhanced by having a clearer framework.

Anxiety remained about how the National Curriculum was to be implemented.

It has been unsatisfactory. The whole thing was set in train in a way we would not have wanted, firstly because it was set out in subjects, and secondly because of the scale and pace of change required.

The LEA has played an essential role in mediating and interpreting what was expected of schools, taking the view that there was no intrinsic difficulty in working with the National Curriculum, though advisers preferred a focus upon programmes of study rather than attainment targets:

... our view is that learning quality lies in the programmes of learn-ing whereas we are worried that teachers may have to identify what is to be tested and work back to the process of teaching.

The 'survival strategies' adopted by the advisers contained within them import-ant principles for approaching implementation of the National Curriculum:

A lot of our strategy had been to reassure teachers that they can't have it all up and running on day 1. They have to look at what is common across the subject documents, for example, the importance of encour-aging children to ask questions rather than expecting them to incul-cate facts, starting from what the children do and know in everyday experience and work outwards from that. Teachers should start with the common processes of learning, rather than doing, 'English' or 'maths' or 'science' in discrete boxes which start at fixed times in the day. It is difficult to get teachers to see, for example, that science is also a language activity because of the importance of accurate descrip-tion, while a visit to a historic building can involve a number of related learning activities: understanding the past, mapping, measure-ment, talking and writing. Teachers should then go to the document to check which learning activities have been completed, which omit-ted. We are encouraging teachers to think of the curriculum as activi-ties and experiences rather than subjects, to be flexible in how they arrange the process of learning so that they have clear objectives for a lesson but are able to respond to children's enquiry.

So we are using the National Curriculum documents as an analytical retrospective checklist. We are saying to teachers, start with activities in a holistic way and then go to the documents to check what has been accomplished ... We want teachers to identify what is good and what they are proud of in practice and to build on what they have been doing. They need to hold on to this, a foundation on which they can build — they must not scrap all that they have been doing and go back to the beginning. That would be fatal.

If a National Curriculum was to be implemented effectively, it required the classroom teacher, the school and the LEA to develop a clear view about what they were trying to achieve in the process of teaching and learning. The curriculum had to be developed bottom up even to accommodate the national framework. Advisers hoped that this would be realized through the process of school development planning which should be curriculum centred and grow out of a realistic assessment of where a school is at and what it can achieve.

The Authority's advisers worked from the outset to meet the need which teachers and schools were expressing for clear guidelines for implementing the National Curriculum. Implementing the National Curriculum forced adviser colleagues to come together and work out a common approach to implementation: a National Curriculum Planning Group and a Curriculum and Assessment team were formed. Anxieties were expressed at the outset about how the separate subjects could all be implemented: but discussion enabled advisers to think through their approach:

> ... at one meeting the geographer was talking about basic skills within the subject and the science adviser said that they were also science skills. It was a seminal moment. It was perceived as a moment when the discussion moved beyond the subject to skills, attitudes and processes. We discovered a lot of agreement.

This encouraged advisers to reexamine the LEA's *Policy Statement on the Curriculum* and to prepare a document for consultation which clarified the principles: the document *On Quality* describes the characteristics of a good school, its curriculum, classroom practice and assessment. It was the subject of widespread discussion and negotiation. While differences of emphasis remained, a shared LEA view began to emerge and shape important policy documents, such as *Planning for Children's Learning in the Primary School*, inform in-service training, and be communicated in county-wide bulletins, as well as talks to governors and parents. Indeed, the county's documents on the National Curriculum and assessment have been regarded as exemplary regionally: they have been very well received: heads find them useful, teachers read them and our HMI tells us he recommends them all over the West Midlands as best practice in the National Curriculum.

### The Need for Partnership between Centre and Locality: A Borough LEA's Experience

The views of officers and advisers in the Midland county were reflected by colleagues in a London borough. This urban LEA also recognized the necessary role of 'the centre'.

> It is important, if you are trying to learn all the time, you have got to expose yourself to as many outside influences as possible. We have always given credit to national developments: to the further education

unit and 'a basis for choice' was an important component in our earlier curriculum thinking; TVEI; the HMI's 'areas of experience', and the DES policy document on science was very good . . . So we have made use of everything we could, but we have kicked against some of the rigidities of the assumptions in the National Curriculum of a subject rather than whole curriculum focus . . . Certainly if it hadn't been for the LEA's insistence on those aspects of the curriculum that run through the different subjects areas, then those would, I think, have been forgotten. The DES is now happy to accept that themes such as interpersonal relationships and social health education exist, but there is a danger that without the Local Authority's experience, they could have been forgotten . . . Given everything we do leads us to collaborative models of learning and development, we are bound not to be able to accept a model which says everything you can do is dictated from the centre: we simply could not live with such a model.

It is not to say that the National Curriculum doesn't have a place as a framework, but as a broad framework. But it is because you need a notion of constant evolutionary development of the curriculum and of education that you also need to have local curriculum development. There is a blind spot at the moment, and I can't see how we could carry on through the middle of the nineties without actually regenerating local curriculum development. To be effective, the curriculum has to be renewed to meet new local needs. But also because teachers and schools have to believe in what they are doing if they are to be successful, and thus to take the glossy documents and tackle the difficult task of thinking it through themselves, to make sense of it . . . Individuals, schools and authorities have to think afresh about problems rather than accept a single orthodoxy . . . No one has a monopoly of the right approach . . . and it is important that the school or the authority continues to assert its individuality and the fact of difference, because otherwise you switch in educational terms to an authoritarian state. The larger the system, the greater the capacity for being wrong on a larger scale.

Local curriculum development has to come back again. After all, one of the reasons why GCSE was implemented so effectively was because a lot of local curriculum development had taken place prior to its construction, a lot of things had happened beforehand. Similarly, with the National Curriculum in science: it came in on the back of all the changes which had been going on in science education locally. So I think that the success of any National Curriculum depends upon the capital of local curriculum development.

The model of change is mistaken. It must not be the mere implementation of something external to us, but rather as harnessing the National Curriculum requirements within the learning model which we are developing. Neither inspection reports nor National

Curriculum documents alone can cause change. Rather it is the pressure which derives from a local authority with a community of professionals working collaboratively across the system with members to develop education to meet identified learning needs.

No government could carry out reforms of the educational system without a local body interested in seeing the best bits of those reforms developed. If there is nothing between the DES and the school, you will build in inertia.

The perspective of a county and a London Borough acknowledge the value of a national framework, but illustrate that effective teaching and learning requires a significant local dimension. Even starting form the subject-based assumptions of the present National Curriculum, its effective realization depends upon teachers, advisers and governors beginning, bottom-up, with clear whole curriculum policies for each school and LEA. The national framework works best as a set of guidelines for the local partners who require increased discretion to exercise their creative contribution.

## Towards 2000 and an Empowered Curriculum

The argument for greater local influence and discretion in curriculum development derives its force from an understanding of the conditions for achievement in schools and classrooms. A number of LEAs have come to believe that if the entrenched disadvantage and underachievement which confronts them is to be diminished, then a new approach is required, one which goes beyond entitlement and equity to empowerment. Achievement will only be enhanced, it is proposed, when motivation is restored. This depends on a vision of teaching and learning which 'transforms the way people think about themselves and what they are capable of'.

The management challenge was perceived by these LEAs to be to draw up a blueprint to enable local people to develop confidence in their own capacity to plan the future development of the communities in which they lived. The main features of these blueprints can be summarized as:

(i)  **Valuing capability**: Values were chosen to celebrate the untapped-reservoirs of capability in individuals: the purpose of education being to create active rather than passive learners, endowed with the skills to make responsible choices about the direction of their own lives as well as to cooperate with others to improve the quality of life for all in the community. This can be broken down into:

(a)  *Valuing the identity and dignity of each*, to develop the self-esteem which is a pre-condition for learning.

(b)  *Belief in individual capacity and achievement*: this is perceived as a pre-condition for learning: 'that no limit should be assumed to the individual's capacity for achievement. This must be the basis of expectations of all children and young people from all backgrounds'.

(c) *Valuing assertiveness and self-confidence*: to learn is to reach out, to go out, to examine something beyond the self; to encounter a different environment and the strangers within it. The value of self-confidence is especially important for those groups — girls, the black and ethnic minorities — which have, traditionally, been disadvantaged in education. The need is acknowledged to develop their self-confidence and assertiveness:

> We want girls to be proud of being female and be aware that they can enter any profession they wish and that they can play a major role both in the school and in the world outside. The school wishes to ensure that girls will leave equipped with the skills to speak up for themselves, to be assertive and to question ... You have this history of girls being passive and seen as well-behaved and 'very good students' because they sit in a corner and read and copy out. But when they are actually tested on paper, they can do poorly. I think passivity is a great danger. Girls unfortunately have a history of being told to shut up while the male speaks, whatever culture they come from. We have got to build up the self-esteem and self-confidence of girls.

Black students, similarly, are encouraged to learn to question and to challenge — their history for example: they have to learn to ask whose history, what history, and whose benefit it is to write this down. What's missing and what's not here.

(d) *Valuing autonomy and responsibility*: this enables children to become independent learners, to manage what they are doing, make decisions about the best way of doing it and to have access to resources. Students need to be able to think and act for themselves so that they can achieve the maximum control over their lives; students need to become self-reliant, self-motivating, able to make decisions for themselves; and to accept responsibility for their actions.

(e) *Valuing responsibility* for others and the wider community: schools and colleges should help young people to form constructive and co-operative attitudes to each other, to their work and to the community so that they can play an active and responsible role in society.

(ii) **Comprehensive curriculum**: The plans sought to develop principles which would encourage a comprehensive curriculum to be developed that would be *relevant* to learners, enabling them to draw upon their experience of living within the community. The curriculum, it was proposed, should be broad and balanced, *modular* in its form, though ensuring *coherence* and integration across the experience of learning, enabling *continuity and progression* in learning, and supporting young people with *formative and positive assessment*.

(iii) **Active learning**: If learning is to be effective, it should motivate young people by engaging their interests and by being related to their experience. 'We must shift from a teaching approach to a learning approach: we must look at what is going on in children's lives, in the community and make the curriculum relevant to their lives.'

The learning process needs to be a more active experience than it has been traditionally in most schools. The pattern familiar to generations, of pupils sitting passively at their desk listening to the teacher and copying from the blackboard, is believed to stifle rather than encourage learning progress. To actively involve the pupils is to engage their interest, to sustain their motivation to succeed . . . encourages students to *take responsibility* for the learning experience of themselves and others.

(a) *Student centred learning*: education should begin from the position and needs of the individual and not merely the benchmarks of preconceived standards. It should start with the positives. We must take time and involve students, to share the ownership of learning. It is only when the child is involved that he or she will really want to learn 'to write' or 'to read'. We need to listen to children.

(b) *Partipation and dialogue*: motivation is more likely if learning grows out of a process of agreeing with pupils the tasks to be undertaken. 'Thus successful learning experiences will stem from negotiating the learning task'.

(c) *Learning by serving others*: learning can be given meaning and purpose by serving the needs of others in the community: it can develop cognitive powers. Community enterprise and community service are illustrations of good practice in themselves, but the idea can be developed within the traditional 'subject' (for example, designing electrical circuitry for use in sheltered flats for the aged so that the warden can be alerted when something is wrong).

(d) *Collaborative learning*: if students are to achieve the educational values of respecting and understanding other persons and cultures, then the very process of learning must encourage collaborative as well as individual activity. Pupils need to be given responsibility to develop projects together so that they decide the ends and plan the means. ('There is too little group work in classrooms ... progress in learning should be a shared activity; we require others to contribute to our discoveries and to support our own development: learning is most fulfilling as a co-operative activity rather than a solitary enterprise, that cooperation is more fruitful than competition.')

(e) *Learning as enjoyment*: 'learning should be interesting and challenging, it should be an exciting experience: it should be fun: too many schools are still boring environments'.

(iv) **Partnership with parents and the community**: Partnership with parents is regarded as a key to improving pupil motivation and achievement while commitment to involvement of the public reflects the broader responsibility of school and college to promote education within the community. One institution had symbolized the partnership with parents by creating a parents' room at the centre of the school: 'we place parents at the centre as prime educators'. Characteristics of partnership for learning quality include:

(a) *Welcoming parents into the life of the school as partners*: establishing a style in which schools will listen to and respond to parents: 'as teachers we need to listen, learn and respect: the great mystique about teacher autonomy needs to be unmasked'.

(b) *Parents as complimentary educators*: the contribution of parents in schemes of reading is encouraged because of its acknowledged influence upon motivation, confidence and attainment scores; one authority has designed a maths package for parents to work on with their children in the home; some heads seek to extend the principle to involving parents in their project-based learning outside the school; while 'portage' schemes promote the mutual responsibilities of the partners in the learning of children with special needs. Schools need to recognize and to harness the wide range of skills and experience amongst parents.

(c) *Developing shared understanding of the curriculum*: the task of establishing a closer match of understanding within the partnership takes time given the differences of perception. But drawing parents in to experience the learning process can develop their confidence in it: '... parents ... need to know what is intended, how it is to be pursued and achieved'.

(d) *Dialogue in curriculum design*: listening to parents and members of the community can bring enrichment to the curriculum both in the subject sense and in areas such as multicultural education.

(e) *Partners in assessment*: establishing regular communication with parents about the progress their child is making; involving the parent in assessment and reaching a shared strategy about future development.

(f)  *Partners in evaluation and accountability*: a school having the confidence to report to parents about performance, and to be genuinely accountable to them. This implies openness and honesty about weaknesses and failures.

What we learn from the LEA blueprint is the significance of a new concept of the purposes and conditions of learning. We cannot learn without being active and motivated; without others (i.e. the support of society); and without shared understanding and agreement about justice, rights and dignity. This suggests that if we are to establish the conditions for disadvantaged communities to flourish, to be motivated and to take their learning and their lives seriously, then a partnership of learning needs to be devised.

## Conclusion

The National Curriculum has been a necessary development establishing the principle of entitlement and securing the values of careful planning and communication. These accomplishments will need time for consolidation. But if the National Curriculum does not allow greater space for the creative participation of the local partners, then its contribution will be partial and incomplete. The right to be taught a subject is a significant development, but the capacity to respond to that opportunity will depend upon the quality of purpose kindled and sustained by the learning environment.

The way forward for the National Curriculum is to articulate more explicitly than hitherto a clearer sense of educational purpose for the times we live in, to release and support the creative energies of LEAs, teachers, governors, parents and communities. This can emerge out of the existing 'theme' documents of the National Curriculum which could be drawn together to express a vision of education for citizenship in the learning society, encouraging all to value their active role as citizens and thus their shared responsibility for the common wealth. Active learning in the classroom needs to be informed by, and lead towards, active citizenship within a participatory democracy.

It is only when the values and processes of learning for citizenship are centrally placed that conditions can be established for all to develop their potential, and institutions can respond imaginatively to change. The transformations of the time require a new valuing of, and commitment to, learning and to partnership. A learning society needs to celebrate the qualities of being open to new ideas, listening to as well as expressing points of view, unearthing by lateral thinking solutions to new dilemmas, participating in change and critically reviewing it. Teachers and educational managers with their deep understanding of the process of learning, can play a leading role in *enabling* such a vision to unfold, not only among young people, but the population as a whole.

## Note

1   This chapter draws upon Ranson (1992).

## References

HMI (1990) *The Implementation of the National Curriculum in Primary Schools*, London, Department of Education and Science.

RANSON, S. (1992) The *Role of Local Government in Education*, London, Longman.

RANSON, S. (forthcoming) *Towards the Learning Society*, London, Cassell.

# Chapter 11

# The Future — Getting Beyond Mastermind in the National Curriculum

*Tim Brighouse*

Our contestants tonight are a Local Government Officer from Clwyd, a teacher from Stockport, a bank clerk from Orpington and a taxi-driver from Coventry. Their specialist subjects are the novels of Raymond Chandler, the paintings of France in the nineteenth century, cricket in Yorkshire in the period 1900 to 1949 and the wives and loves of Henry VIII. Now may we have the first contestant please . . .

This chapter will argue that the National Curriculum started with the disadvantage of being designed within a cultural context too heavily dominated by knowledge transfer and acquisition so that there was from the start a lack of balance among information, skills, and ideas. It will also maintain that the knowledge explosion, coupled with the fateful decisions both to start with a framework of subjects and to design the subjects one by one, rather than initially, as a whole led to overload and overcomplexity in designs. It takes these design faults, as well as the basic calibration of testing with 'levels' as given, but argues for a solution by suggesting that the curriculum should be seen as four separate but interrelated dimensions: the National Curriculum, the school curriculum combining both timetabled and non-timetabled activity, the home curriculum and personal curriculum.

HMI asked for a 'broad', 'balanced' 'coherent' curriculum: indeed those three words, which represented the growing professional consensus of the 1970s and the 1980s are perhaps appropriate criteria by which to judge the efficacy of the early experience of the National Curriculum. Superficially, the proponents at the time of its introduction argued that the three core and seven foundation subjects, together with the legally-required religious education, represented such *breadth, balance and coherence*. It is, of course, difficult to know what HMI actually thought about the legislated proposals because they were, by that time, too closely involved in its introduction and it was, after all, essentially a politically-inspired design: but it isn't too difficult to guess that they found some strain in reconciling what was essentially a very traditional and anachronistic view of the curriculum with their own more thoughtful approaches involving areas of experience and some of the ideas expressed in the *Curriculum Matters* series.

In practice, the National Curriculum has so far lacked true *balance* and coherence and one of the main tasks of those who will wish to reform it will be to put right its design flaws. Once it had been decided that the *whole* of the curriculum would not be debated before *each* of the individual subjects, it was in any case inevitable that *coherence* and *balance* would be sacrificed. Where subjects overlap, as they inevitably do, those which were considered first would claim particular pre-eminence in matters, whether affecting information, skills, attitudes or ideas, about which they, the subject specialists, felt strongly. The territorial ambitions of academic generalists in the fields of humanities and social science, for example, are to be compared with the most rampant imperialist in the political history of Great Britain, France, Spain, Germany and Portugal, over the last 400 years in Europe, Africa and America. The scarcely veiled scorn and disdain mutually exhibited in higher education bears testimony to the increased balkanization inevitable with the march in the expansion of knowledge. Moreover, a moment's reflection on the phrase 'my subject needs', so often heard at the time of timetable consultation in secondary schools, explains the inevitability of overdesign once the political decision was taken to design subject by subject rather than overall.

No mechanism was set up by the Secretary of State of the time, either to provide an initial or, at second best, an ongoing overview as each report came in. Certainly it must have been painfully clear to the National Curriculum Council that such was needed as well as some system of umpiring disputes between specialist lobbies. Indeed, after the scurry of the first few months, when the urgent necessity of the timetable brooked no arguments and when it had little time for broader reflection, the NCC sought to retrieve the situation through its committee framework and its excellent 'curriculum guidance' series. Indeed, in providing an overview and in seeking to make sense of the cross-curricular themes, issues and skills, the documents in the series are the most valuable to emerge from the whole planning and implementation exercise. The incoherence and lack of balance is evident, however, to anyone who has sought to carry out the now fashionable audit of each subject in search, for example, of *environmental education* or, more elusively, *citizenship*, as a cross-curricular theme. In the summer terms of 1991 and 1992, with sixteen PGCE students based in two Stoke-on-Trent high schools, I sought, as their tutor and with the help of the two Deputy Headteachers, to carry out such audits. The task, which has been enormously time-consuming but fun, has led on each occasion to a display of the themes and the beginnings of school policies on the issues. One was left, however, doubtful about the practicability of similar exercises unaided by outsiders and the way in which the cross-curricular elements would be taken forward for the future. The imperatives of the core and foundation subjects, after all, are stern: the 'my subject needs' syndrome remains a powerful antidote to cross-curricular action.

Indeed, once *subjects* as such had been decided as the main strand for

National Curriculum design, there was likely to be an over-emphasis on information at the expense of skills, attitudes and concepts: and as such it is at the very heart of another problem of the grand design. The generation in charge of the design, inevitably in middle age, experienced a higher education which laid — indeed until very recently continued to lay — enormous stress on a narrow range of skills and knowledge. They were bound to be affected by that experience. After all, the pattern of the university and polytechnic course has continued to be one which demands the recall of *surface* learning rather than *deeper* understanding. The difference between a first and third class degree illustrates the point clearly. The former, when analyzed through answers in final examinations, reveals a candidate who can demonstrate analysis and synthesis of reading coupled with some personal and appropriate critical engagement with the material. The latter, on the other hand, sometimes shows little more than an incoherent regurgitation of more or less related facts. There are implications here for appropriate methods of assessment — i.e. terminal in preference to continuous — but it is the backwash effect of the system on the balance among information, skills, attitudes and concepts, which I first wish to examine as a National Curriculum fault.

The point is already made that the National Curriculum's preoccupation with information acquisition at the expense of other parts of the curriculum was a reflection of earlier generations' own education, overlaid with political necessity. Donald Naismith, a maverick Education Officer credited with considerable political influence on Conservative thinking, was similarly driven. His son's failure to have heard of Oliver Cromwell was, according to Naismith, the reason he introduced a curriculum for Croydon — a step which is said to have hastened the introduction of the National Curriculum after the White Paper, *Better Schools*, less than two years before its actual introduction, had suggested a statutory backing for the curriculum was not in the politicians' mind. In an ironic and bizarrely trivial fashion, the story of Naismith echoes one attributed to Robert Lowe, the architect of the curriculum which was to be the benchmark for the period of payment by results. When his eyesight was failing, he is said to have been so outraged when children summoned from the streets failed to be able to read polysyllabic words for him that he settled on simple reading as a crucial part of the Revised Code.

To some extent, Magnus Magnusson and his compulsive show, *Mastermind*, represent the modern view of education. Essentially, the show puts the participants under great pressure to reveal facts unaided by anything but memory, prodigious in scope and lightning fast in operation. Even the second round repeats the format, but this time to recall accurately 'general knowledge'. Most contemporary game shows linked to substantial prizes have the basic ingredient — information allied to speed of retrieval. The popular parlour game, *Trivial Pursuit* relies on the same formula minus the pressure.

The common idea of education which prevails today, reduced to shape and practices of a set of trucks all in a row, memory trucks with navvies pitching ballast into them against time or not doing so as the case may be. Yet loading up people's minds with other people's facts is not educating minds . . . (letter to *The Times*, 1886)

So wrote Thring more than a century ago. The media programmes, *University Challenge, Brain of Britain, Top of the Form, Mastermind. A Question of Sport*, all have underlying them a similarity to the 'common idea of education' to which Thring objected. It is essentially and predominantly a transmission model of education. As Mrs Thatcher once said. 'We must not only know what our children are expected to know, but we must know whether they have learnt it'.

Such a view of the curriculum, with its heavy emphasis on factual recall, probably has its roots in the dim and distant past before printing, when the aura of transmission of vital and limited information was essential to a society's continuing economic and cultural survival. Indeed, the very word *lecturer* and the continuing heavy reliance on the *lecture* as the standard form of delivery in higher education echoes the habits of the ancient universities before the ready availability of the printed word! The more recent transformation of the means of retreiving and handling knowledge represented by advances in information technology must surely render the old models and balance towards information invalid. Information and knowledge is there aplenty: it is knowing how to retrieve it and use it wisely which is the more important aspect of knowledge. 'Deep' rather than 'surface' learning is called for.

The point has already been made about the unfortunate backwash effect of higher education on the schooling system as a whole and by inference on the methods deployed in the education of those for whom higher education will always remain inaccessible. For so long, therefore, as there continues to be a dominant reliance of the 'final' examination in higher education without the aid of reference books, justified by models similar to that at 'A' level, there will continue to be the problem of bias towards *information* in the curriculum and recall of surface information in assessment. It is a view which stands as a large inhibition to those engaged in curriculum innovation and experiments. To the person in the street, however, and the parent alike, the language of professional educators seems unnecessarily jargonistic and inaccessible. So most of the decade from Callaghan's Ruskin speech to the Red Consultation Paper of 1987 was taken up by headteachers, teachers, specialists, advisers and inspectors debating among themselves under the leadership of HMI a more sophisticated interpretation of the curriculum which was on a plain quite removed from the politician, the parent and the busy classroom teacher alike.

When Mr Baker, therefore, imposed the 1987 self-styled Great Education Reform Bill, there was not much grass roots opposition to the actual curriculum definition nor to the list of three core and seven foundation subjects. Some of the mockery was confined to those who espoused a new subject, 'technology'.

Perhaps what is catching all of us out and what may yet provide a key capable of unlocking our unjustified faith in a 'mastermind' curriculum is the recent explosion of knowledge. There is simply more information to know. One of the reasons, perhaps, that the curriculum remained so static and unaltered for the first half of the century was that knowledge expanded relatively slowly even if rapidly by comparison with previous centuries.

Therefore, even if the curriculum had been planned as a whole, it would have still been the case that the sum of the parts within a subject and between subjects would inevitably be greater than could be accommodated within a normal school day, school year and child's school career! The temptation to put too much in, given the knowledge explosion, is irresistible. Indeed, the most obvious 'quart into a pint pot' argument surfaced early during the discussions about Key Stage 4 — its urgency highlighted by the implications for the public examination system at 16. The compromise which ensued split the lobby of a 'broad balanced curriculum': part of the influence of the compromise was opinion expressed privately by the headteachers of independent schools attended by the children of cabinet ministers and who felt obliged to keep up with the general thrust of the National Curriculum and its assessment arrangements and could recognise its indigestibility. They could not comply and still capitalize on children with remarkable facility in languages or science at age 14. The overdesign, however, is even clearer in the earlier stages during the primary years, where the lobby, however articulate, is barely heard. Perhaps there are fewer influential connections to help its advocacy. Teachers who are responsible for the curriculum both of 5, 6 and 7-year-olds (Key Stage 1) and, more obviously, of 8, 9, 10 and 11-year-olds (Key Stage 2) wonder how they can include all that it implied within *all* of the three core and six (modern language of course comes later) foundation subjects within the time available while still attempting to deal with the complexities of every child's reading development not to mention the emotional problems which some children bring to school from a more diverse and less tightly coupled society.

Beyond the point of *over-ambitious* design and lop-sided bias towards *knowledge*, the first years of the National Curriculum have been stymied by the *over-complicated* and *over-detailed* nature of the original prescription. How far this was politically driven in the preferred outcome of the task group on assessment and testing (TGAT) has not been revealed. Nevertheless, teachers — even the most energetic and enthusiastic of them — have been cumulatively weighed down by the avalanche of paperwork, most of it caused by too close a theoretical adherence in the original design to Bloom's Taxonomy. In consequence, at first there were as many as seventeen attainment targets for science and fifteen for maths: no sooner, however, had teachers wrestled with the task of designing a system for recording both their coverage of the attainment targets and their recording of their pupils' progress towards the achievement of these targets in the assessment arrangements, than there was a redesign towards a more manageable and lesser number of attainment targets. The resulting redesign is more effective in addressing the presentational than the substance of overcomplicated design. Not much has been dropped. What is to be done to solve these three problems — the undue bias towards information;

the appetite of the National Curriculum to get even larger; and the over-complication of design, all underpinned by inappropriate assessment, the design of which is separated from the curriculum?

The odds against solving it are enormous. To some extent, the reform of the GCSE, with its express intent to establish what candidates 'knew', 'understood' and 'could do' was a step in the right direction, reinforced by an increased dependence on 'coursework' as a vital means of assessment. It shifted the balance away from information. Nevertheless, its initial gains were politically unacceptable: in consequence, during 1991/92 there was a decision to reverse the trend and reduce the proportion of coursework assessment in GCSE assessment. In a similar fashion, the attempts of the TGAT group to give priority to teacher assessment of children's progress at the end of each key stage were eventually frustrated. It will be recalled that the original SATs were to be means of moderating teacher assessment. The move, however, towards simplicity and shortened tests will emphasize what pupils 'know' at the expense of what they 'understand' and 'can do'. To complete this depressing picture, the feature of the UK education scene with the most intractability to resist reform seems to be the 'A' level examination. Despite the efforts of the reformers, 'A' level remains the most profligate consumer of human talent with its 30–40 per cent wastage and failure rates. To this day, those whom the 'A' level system serves — of course the universities and colleges, not the students — have seen it as a useful filler and have used the expected grades at 'A' level as a mechanism for entry to higher education, even though the correlation between 'A' level grade and university degree performance is slight.

There is, however, some room for optimism and the source of it comes from higher education which, as I have argued, traditionally has produced a powerful backwash effect on the schools. Almost unnoticed, the universities are embarking on a sea change in their own curriculum and assessment design. Moves to modularization and a semester system, together with credit transfer, are now past the point of no return. More than a dozen universities plan to have their courses planned and delivered on a modular basis by 1993. Such moves demand a review of the traditional 'finals' system of assessment, which in turn calls for an examination by course designers of the questions of progression and of what, beyond surface learning, they are seeking to assess. Gradually there emerges a healthy debate about the whole curriculum, albeit for a fairly selective group of students, but in higher education there is no party political interference, as there has been in the school's field, to prejudice or preempt the outcome of the debate. In the longer run this revolution — for such it is — will mean that higher education will rely less on 'A' level, which, as we have seen, is an unreliable predictor but more on a profile of achievement, if not for their national competition for entry, at least for their quota of applicants finding access to higher education through locally-designed routes. They will do so because they will be less concerned about what aspiring students know on the surface and more about their capacity to handle knowledge and their wider talents. Then, perhaps, we shall be able to revive the debates, so profitably promoted by HMI in the late 1970s, for a redesigned framework for the schools curriculum so that the emphasis among information, skills, attitudes, concepts is less lop-sided, less inclined towards surface rather than deeper learning and more balance, as between the individual parts.

If that promises the solution to the information overload of the curriculum, what is to be done about its size?

Just as a national Government in Westminster fails against the unnecessarily detailed requirements of the European Commission and argues the case for 'subsidiarity', so, as we have seen, do schools creak under the detailed weight of curricular national prescription. Sometimes, too, the scale is confusingly wrong to the hard-pressed teacher, the national design seems occasionally to put footpath detail, as it were, on a motorway map. A group of Oxfordshire headteachers spotted the need to get the *scale* right as between *external* and *internal* design when they urged the Education Committee in 1986, in the wake of the Education Act of that year which required the LEA to have a curriculum policy, 'to ensure that the LEA's promised curriculum statement should be only so thick as would enable it to be slipped under a closed door'! It is difficult to see, given the political appetite for central prescription, how this confusion of scale can be reversed. There may be a solution by arguing for the curriculum to be seen as four dimensional.

Perhaps we need to rethink our definition of the *whole curriculum*. We have a *National Curriculum* which we have seen as too large. If there were to be a debate about the need for the *school* curriculum, a *home* curriculum, and a *personal* curriculum and how each related to the other, it might be possible to chart a solution to the problem. Consider.

We have already discussed the flaws of the National Curriculum, particularly in respect of its over-design — and some would say its inappropriate subject-driven framework. If the school were required, for argument's sake, to adopt 70 per cent of its overall 'timetabled curriculum' from that specified nationally both within and between subjects, there would be left to the school the capacity for each subject teacher to choose within his or her subject the remaining 30 per cent of subject matter; such subject matter could be chosen either from the nationally-available curriculum, or be 'own design'. Similarly, the school itself might also decide 30 per cent of its *timetabled* curriculum either from the nationally available curriculum or from its own initiative. The legitimacy of both could, of course, be accredited (or not) during the four-yearly regular external inspections of schools required under the 1992 Education (Schools) Act.

Schools will interpret this freedom in different ways: some will play safe and settle for the national detail, while others will have two timetables — one devoted, perhaps, to three terms each of ten weeks with the balance of eight weeks in the year used to reinforce cross-curricular themes, topics and skills on a totally different timetabled basis. Yet others might want to use the eight weeks differently, for example by capitalizing on the enthusiasms of particular teachers to pursue geology or philosophy or psychology or yet other disciplines represented in higher education and therefore within the knowledge compass of enthusiastic teachers but now excluded from the school's curriculum.

Within the school, however, there will be more than the *timetabled* curriculum; there will be the vital but misnamed extra-curricular activities, many of which are more important than conventional timetable. The diversity of lunchtime/after school clubs and societies will be supplemented by activities ranging across drama, music, sport, outdoor activity, theatre and film visits, together with residential trips and in and out of school community service. Within what, in effect, would be the voluntary, as opposed the the compulsory, aspect of the school curriculum, there would be room to exert peer group pressure of the right sort towards achievement. The school curriculum would be defined globally in such terms and the school would be required to give an account and demonstrate the coherence, breadth and balance of its particular pattern both of the timetabled compulsory and the non-timetabled voluntary curriculum during the visits of the four-yearly inspectors.

The *home* curriculum — a third category of curriculum beyond the national and the school's — would be the outcome of the home/school partnership: as such it would represent the cornerstone of the learning relationship among pupil, teacher and parents. This element of the curriculum will help to emphasize the key role of the parents as educators — beyond those of consumer, manager and captive supporter which present market-driven forces tend to emphasize. So the *home* curriculum would start at birth with the mother and the health visitor: it would proceed through pre-school years involving a judicious mixture of experiences within the home and in voluntary and statutory provisions, so that there would be a clear expectation of youngsters arriving at the compulsory ages of schooling already able to take advantage of the education available, indeed of the *school* curriculum. From the beginning — at age 5 — until the end of compulsory schooling — at age 16 — the interplay of the *home* and the *school* curriculum within the *national* framework is vital and will vary from student to student according to their various and changing needs as they develop. Hence there is a need for a *personal* curriculum — a carefully charted personal progress in the form of a record of achievement which becomes the vital vehicle of continuity. Breadth, balance and coherence, therefore, become something not achieved continuously and simultaneously by the student, but over time by age 16, or preferably 19 or 20. The particular mix at any one time of the three core and seven foundation subjects, of the timetabled and non-timetabled school curriculum, of the home curriculum, will be a matter designed to capture the fire and enthusiasm of the youngster, their teachers and parents. Success and confidence will flow from personal motivation. Coherence to the student is a very mysterious and personal matter. The *personal* curriculum is therefore vital. It is the thread which interweaves the other ingredients — the *national*, the *school* and the *home*.

Unfortunately, for this to be turned into reality requires a shift in assessment arrangements. That, however, may not be such an unrealistic demand as it may sound; for the two year developmental delay between each *level* of the statements of attainment, may, with the benefit of hindsight, be a major mistake. It is scarcely likely to be motivational to the pupil: moreover it is certain in practice to reveal a disturbing lack of pupil progress from the parents' point of view between successive annual school reports and especially in the difficult years between 8, 11 and 14. All this might add impetus, perhaps in the name of simplification, to a demand for an overhaul of the assessment arrangements. If the levels were to be retained but completed after recalibration between ages 11 and 14 we should restore more differentiation, motivation — at a crucial time — and a sense of progression.

If the assessment of the National Curriculum as we know it were finished by age 14 and succeeded by a series of modular assessments designed to ensure achievement of breadth and balance by age 19 we should have a basis for matriculation requirements for entry into trades, professions and higher education which would more closely match their needs. Such a profile achieved by that age would be a combination of the vocational and academic.

Prior to embarking on such a 14–19 set of courses, a student would therefore achieve a score at age 14 expressed as a points score (e.g. 5.6 or 4.2) and it would be possible to demand a basic minimum score required in the core and other foundation subjects. Those who achieve less than the specified figure would carry on with their basic work in the core subjects whilst simultaneously embarking for the rest of their timetabled curriculum on the modular courses designed to capture their flagging interest at a most difficult time.

Earlier, the assessments at 7 must be so geared as to require the teachers to identify each child as good in at least some activity. Thring once said that 'All children have it within them to walk a step or two of the way with genius': if we haven't identified that step by age seven, the ebbing confidence and lack of success that a child experiences is likely to mean that the step will never happen.

What I have attempted to show so far is how is may be possible to accept 'what is' — warts and all — and proceed to 'what might be'.

Finally, however, and for that to happen, there is some structural change required in planning at the national level. The separation of the planning of the curriculum from the assessment arrangements is illogical. Apart from the thinly-veiled rivalry which the National Curriculum Council (NCC) and the Schools Examination Assessment Council (SEAC) have indulged in, there are few, if any, precedents for perpetuating separation. There are two reasons for the separation, and both are difficult to justify. The first is the precedent created by the prior existence of the Schools Curriculum Development Committee (SCDC) and the Secondary Examination Council (SEC), which had been created as replacements for the politically unpopular and abolished Schools' Council. Prior to that, of course, the various GCE boards had approved syllabuses for assessment purposes at 'O' and 'A' levels. Basically, the latter phenomenon leads to the second reason, namely the existence of the secondary public exam system being founded on a mistrust of teachers' honesty or capability. The separation of the teacher from the syllabus design and still more the means of assessment deprives the teacher of a sense of ownership or certainty of the direction which the learning of the children is meant to take. Where assessment and curriculum design work were combined, for example in Mode 3 syllabuses, there has been historically much more enthusiasm amongst teachers. Indeed, teachers wishing to improve their own pupils' performance at GCSE have always traditionally sought to involve themselves in GCSE marking in order to combine in their own minds their criteria for assessment with their own everyday teaching techniques. All successful teachers know, in every lesson they teach, that there is certain information and skills they want their pupils to learn and concepts which they would have them understand. If they wish to know whether they have been successful in teaching, they will devise the assessment arrangements designed to ascertain whether the lesson has been effective. That is what universities do: they have one internal agency and committee which vets not merely the examination system, but also the proposals for new courses. In a sense, therefore, assessment always wags the curriculum dog. It has been fashionable because of the GCE experience for teachers to agree that they regret that that is the case — as though it could be otherwise. Ultimately, as I have, however, explained, it is the hallmark of good teaching and learning. The sooner, therefore, at national level, that the two are acknowledged as inseparable and combined in the organization and the design of the National Curriculum and Assessment arrangements the better. Then, perhaps, we should have a single body which would devote all its energies to solving the problems which have emerged so far in the design.

The agenda I would urge on them is not a root and branch upheaval, nor a return to the 'status quo ante' but a new and different way of looking at the curriculum and assessment.

# Chapter 12

# Common Sense:
# A Programme for the Future

*Michael Barber and Duncan Graham*

The case for a National Curriculum is now undisputed. How can the present one be reformed so that its benefits are maximized and its flaws, whether in design or implementation, ironed out? This brief final chapter is intended to show how that process can be begun. We believe we have drawn on threads of arguments which run throughout the book: much of the justification for our programme therefore is not repeated here. We hope its focussed proposals will generate some worthwhile debate.

## A Framework for Revision

The NCC or its successors body, proposed in current legislation, for School Curriculum and Assessment Authority (SCAA) should publish a document outlining a framework for the curriculum as a whole and a plan for its revision: it should take forward the advice offered in Curriculum Guidance 3 (NCC, 1989). This document should be the subject of a major consultation exercise. It should propose which parts of the existing curriculum subjects should form a non-negotiable core, and which might be optional at the discretion of schools. While most attainment targets would remain, areas of programmes of study could constitute the optional elements. After due debate, there could emerge a slimmed down compulsory core, and elements of choice. The plan should set a precedent by being submitted to ministers, only after the process of proposal, consultation and recommendation is complete. It should be the first step towards establishing the principle that the NCC or SCAA should carry out necessary subject revisions openly and in partnership with all those with a vested interest.

In taking up his post as Chairman and Chief Executive of the National Curriculum Council in 1988, Duncan Graham anticipated that responsibility for the revision of the National Curriculum, once it was in place, would lie with the NCC. It was expected that the NCC would make proposals for revision on the basis of its own evaluations and independently commissioned research. The proposals would then form the basis of an open consultation exercise.

In practice revisions to date have not followed this pattern. In the case of maths and science, the revision of the attainment targets was assessment driven and undertaken behind closed doors in great haste by a group of HMI. A similar process is now in danger of being applied to technology. In the case of English the revision seems to be politically motivated and not based on analytical evaluation of the impact of the Orders in schools. Those charged with revision in technology are clearly working to tight political instructions. This approach if allowed to continue will undermine the credibility of the National Curriculum and compromise its contribution to raising standards.

Revisions should, and must, involve genuine consultation with a wide range of interested parties, not least teachers whose understanding of the implementation of the Orders in practice ought to be considered an essential ingredient of sensible reform.

The NCC would have to take account of the balance of advantage to be gained from making improvements, as against adding to the workload of teachers and pupils. This does not appear to have been considered when maths and science were tackled. There would too be the need to avoid the 'lame-duck' syndrome which has come from the clumsy handling of technology revisions, without consultation, and with untested assumptions and prejudices leaked to the press.

A slimmed down core would provide at school level a real opportunity for the good cross-curricular work which is necessary but has, given the pressure of events, fallen off the bottom of the list of priorities. Duncan Graham's dream of a school throwing the Attainment Targets into the air and re-organizing them as they fell, thus breaking traditional barriers between subjects, might then become a reality.

## The Role of Politicians

If anyone was ever naive enough to believe that education was not a political football, the last decade will have disabused them. Clearly it is. Nevertheless, we believe the extent of political direction in curriculum matters has become excessive in the last three years. Ideally the role of politicians should be limited by statute: if this is impossible there should be hammered out an agreed code of practice which should include the following:

  (i)   how teachers teach should remain a professional matter to be decided at school level in consultation with parents and governors;
  (ii)  politicians should not engage in details of content;
        Kenneth Baker and John MacGregor recognized unwritten rules of this kind. Kenneth Clarke did not. John Patten has also yielded to temptation. Once detailed interference becomes the norm, consistency

in the National Curriculum, so important for its successful implementation, will become unobtainable. The threat to democracy should also be recognized: no-one surely wants a politically tainted National Curriculum.

(iii) Appointments to the NCC and SEAC (and the successor body) should not be the sole preserve of the Secretary of State. If the idea of representation of interests can no longer be entertained, then either appointments should be made by the Privy Council, or they should be subject to approval by the House of Commons Select Committee on Education, Science and the Arts. In any event ministers should refrain from the appointment of those whose political connections manifestly outweigh their experience or knowledge of education.

(iv) All changes in curriculum and assessment policy should be the subject of proposals and consultations undertaken by the NCC or SEAC. They should not emanate exclusively from the Secretary of State.

### The Roles of the NCC, SEAC and NCVQ

The NCC's role should be strengthened to include, as suggested earlier, responsibility for the revision of the National Curriculum. It should be seen as a centre of curriculum expertise and excellence. It should have an independent research budget to assist it in keeping the curriculum under review, free of political constraint.

The respective roles of the NCC, SEAC and NCVQ should be re-examined. Whether three bodies are necessary is questionable. The merger of SEAC and the NCVQ is one possibility, another would be that of NCC and SEAC. It is regrettable that the government has plumped for the latter without due debate on the alternatives. Whether bodies emerge should have executive powers, independent members, and their own research budgets, free from political manipulation.

### Investment

The implementation of the National Curriculum in its revised form should be independently costed. If the Coopers and Lybrand research examined in John Atkin's chapter is not accepted then the Government should commission work of its own. This could beneficially draw on the expertise of the Audit Commission in this field. The NCC and SEAC should make clear the educational assumptions, e.g. on class sizes, upon which costings would be based. Government acknowledgment that successful implementation of reform requires increased investment is long overdue.

### Cross-curricular Themes

The five documents on cross-curricular themes should be brought up-to-date, extended and republished in a single volume. Widely welcomed across the teaching profession and beyond, they would have much greater impact now when the subject orders have been decided and when a less detailed and hopefully more liberal National Curriculum is being discussed. They should not be marginalized or shoved under the 'subject' carpet.

The potential for the development of equal opportunities under the National Curriculum should be exploited. A guide of good practice on the multicultural approaches possible under the National Curriculum should be published; the differential impact of the National Curriculum on girls and boys should be monitored. Research should monitor the progress made by students from different backgrounds: the results of research should form the basis of rethinking policy where necessary.

### Special Educational Needs

There is evidence that the National Curriculum is extending expectations of students with special educational needs and that refreshingly few schools are disapplying the National Curriculum from such students.

This is a prime area for effective evaluative research into the impact of the National Curriculum. While the entitlement it provides is likely to be of benefit, the assessment arrangements could be damaging. Students with special educational needs are likely in many cases to make little or no progress through the ten levels. Subject to the outcomes of detailed research we would suggest that the programmes of study be viewed as an entitlement and that the assessment arrangements be more flexible and take more account of pupils with special educational needs; work on records of achievement and profiles may be relevant in this context.

### Assessment

John Patten's announcement that Key Stage 3 tests in English should include a Shakespeare play has caused some debate. We have no objection to Shakespeare being part of the curriculum of KS3 English. We take exception to the National Curriculum being effectively altered through the design of tests. When the assessment tail wags the curriculum dog, look out for trouble! Booklists are an example of something to be avoided.

Assessment requirements should not dictate the shape of the curriculum. Instead, where necessary the assessment arrangements should be altered to become compatible with the curriculum. Teacher assessment should be the main form of assessment with SATs used to moderate and confirm teachers' judgments, as is already the case in technology. The Scottish Office has implemented proposals very much along these lines. There is room for a demonstration of real trust in teachers. Schools could be accredited to carry out testing to nationally agreed standards.

### In-service Education and the National Curriculum

As Bill Lahr's chapter makes clear, LEAs have made a huge contribution to National Curriculum implementation. If the evidence of research on implementation of major reform (see chapter 2) it to be taken seriously, this kind of role will need to be sustained for several more years. There are three key issues. Firstly, sufficient money needs to be invested in National Curriculum training for teachers. This means at least maintaining present levels through to 1997. Secondly, if LEA advisory services and support teams vanish attention needs to be given to finding alternative delivery mechanisms. This issue, like so many others, appears to have been ignored by the Government as it reflects on the future role of LEAs. Thirdly, there is the question of quality: this means enabling teachers who have successfully grappled with National Curriculum problems to become trainers of others: and it means ensuring teachers have sufficient time to spend on their own professional development. Appraisal should help in giving higher priority to teachers' own learning; but it will not bring about the desired changes unless time and money are invested in meeting the training and other needs thus identified.

### Conclusion

The National Curriculum could become the single most important education reform of the later twentieth century. It could make a substantial contribution to raising standards for all pupils. Whether it does or not, will depend upon the decisions taken by politicians and others involved in the process. During the next two years or so, the curriculum must be reviewed and current shortcomings addressed. If in the process partnerships and trust are fostered, then pupils, parents, commerce, the Government and teachers, can begin to feel that it 'belongs' to them. Only then will it be by definition and in reality a truly National Curriculum.

# Notes on Contributors

**Duncan Graham** CBE was Chairman and Chief Executive of the National Curriculum Council from its establishment in 1988 until July 1991. Prior to that he was successively Chief Education Officer in Suffolk and Chief Executive of Humberside County Council.

In his capacity at the NCC he has had a major influence over the shape of the National Curriculum and unparalleled insight into the process of its implementation. He is now an Education Consultant and visiting Professor at the University of Manchester.

**Michael Barber** is currently Head of the Education and Equal Opportunities Department at the National Union of Teachers. Prior to that he was a teacher and Chair of the Education Committee in Hackney. He is the author of a number of articles and books on educational themes.

**John Atkins** is a consultant with Coopers and Lybrand's Management Consultancy Services, where he specialises in reviews of education and training management and delivery.

**Anne-Marie Bathmaker** is TVEI co-ordinator with responsibility for Equal Opportunities, Walsall.

**Tim Brighouse** is Research Machines Professor of Education at the University of Keele. He was formerly Chief Education Officer for Oxfordshire.

**Elaine Foster** is headteacher of Handsworth Wood Girls' School, Birmingham.

**Alan Leech** is Headteacher of Bohunt Community Comprehensive School, Liphook, Hampshire.

**Stewart Ranson** is Professor of Education, University of Birmingham.

**David Tytler** As Education Editor of *The Times* from 1988 to 1992, David Tytler reported on the introduction of the National Curriculum and its effect on schools. He now writes regularly for both *The Times* and the *Guardian*.

**Anne Waterhouse** has been Headteacher of Asmall County Primary School since January 1984 and is a member of Executive of the National Union.

**Jennifer Wisker** is Chief Education Officer for Somerset County Council, and a member of several bodies including the National Curriculum Council, the Somerset Training and Enterprise Council and she is Chair of the National Youth Agency.

# Name Index

# Subject Index

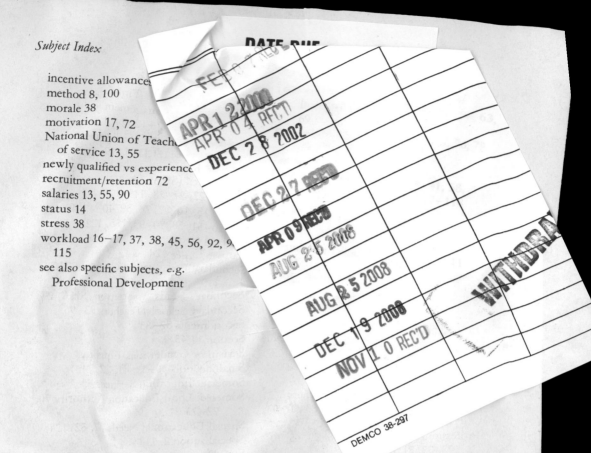